Perfect English Cottage

Perfect English Cottage

Ros Byam Shaw

with photography by **Jan Baldwin**

RYLAND
PETERS
& SMALL

LONDON NEW YORK

This book is dedicated to Lizzy.

Senior designer Toni Kay

Editors Delphine Lawrance
& Clare Double

Location research Ros Byam Shaw
& Emily Westlake

Production Hazel Kirkman

Art director Leslie Harrington

Publishing director Alison Starling

First published in 2009
by Ryland Peters & Small
20–21 Jockey's Fields,
London WC1R 4BW
and
519 Broadway, 5th Floor
New York, NY 10012

10 9 8 7 6 5 4 3

Library of Congress Cataloging-in-
Publication Data

Byam Shaw, Ros.
  Perfect English cottage / Ros Byam
Shaw.
     p. cm.
  Includes index.
  ISBN 978-1-84597-904-1
  1. Cottages--England. 2. Interior
decoration--England. 3. Decoration
and ornament, Rustic--England.
I. Title.
  NK2195.R87B93 2009
  747--dc22

2009015977

A CIP record for this book is available
from the British Library.

Printed and bound in China

CONTENTS

'The cottage homes of England!
By thousands on her plains,
They are smiling o'er the silvery brooks
And round the hamlet fanes.'

FELICIA DOROTHEA HEMANS (1793–1835)

INTRODUCTION

The word 'cottage' is surrounded by a rosy glow. Add 'English' and the glow becomes a little rosier. All the connotations are good. We think small and cosy, rural and peaceful, simple and modest, pretty as the picture on a tin of toffees. We exhale a sigh of relaxation; a cottage means a holiday, escapism, nostalgia.

England is stuffed with lovely cottages in an array of appealing vernacular styles. There are the plump curves of cob and thatch in Devon, the black and white timber frames of Herefordshire, the wavering stripes of Kentish weatherboarding, the golden gables of the Cotswolds and the knobbly flints and russet brick of Norfolk. Dartmoor cottages feature giant slabs of granite, Cornish cottages have fat walls of layered slate, while pantiles exported from the Low Countries undulate over East Anglian cottage roofs.

The cult of the cottage has a long history. In the second half of the 18th century, such was the attraction of the idealized cottage and the simple, wholesome life it seemed to promise that fake cottages became the height of chic. Thirty years after Marie Antoinette played at being a shepherdess in her reproduction hamlet in the grounds of Versailles, Endsleigh

in Devon was built as the grandest *cottage orné* of them all, a stately home gabled and mullioned like a house on the village green. Later in the century, Arts and Crafts architects modified and aggrandized elements of cottage design, and the same stylistic thread runs through much suburban architecture to the present day, when codified 'cottage' is the style of choice for new housing developments in towns, villages and on the edge of cities.

Today's cottage can be as comfortable and convenient as it is enchanting to look at. But this was not always so. The sentimental verses quoted on page 7 were parodied some years later in *Punch* magazine:

'The cottage homes of England!
Alas! How strong they smell;
There's fever in the cesspool
And sewage in the well'

Despite being persistently romanticized, the genuine as opposed to gentrified cottage of the past was more likely to be a slum than a desirable residence. While a rustic confection of thatch and sticks shrouded under a heavy cloak of ivy might look adorable in a painting or as a feature in a landscape garden, the reality of life in such tumbledown shacks was inevitably squalid. A report on the 'Sanitary Conditions of the Labouring Population' presented to Parliament in 1842 was a miserable litany of open sewers, leaking roofs, windows stuffed with rags, mud floors and whole families occupying one room – a far cry from the fragrant images of girls in sun-bonnets, standing at the gates of delphinium-fringed country abodes in the watercolours of popular Victorian artist Helen Allingham.

The use of the word 'cottage' to denote a humble dwelling dates back to Chaucer. However, the generally understood meaning of the word has changed in the last 100 years as standards of housing have radically improved. The hovels inhabited by 'cottagers', who were labourers with no land other than a smallholding, were so flimsy and badly built that most collapsed or were demolished long ago. The buildings that have survived, and which we now call cottages, would have been considered substantial, respectable residences by comparison. Like Monk's House in Part One, they were owned by craftsmen and tradesmen, carpenters, blacksmiths, wheelwrights and bakers, families prosperous enough to have a house with more than one room and more than one storey. Even these relatively well-built homes were sometimes extremely small and the modern cottage, again like Monk's House, is frequently the result of a row of two or more of them knocked into one.

This book features examples of many types of cottage, from the humble Victorian farm worker's cottage of Sara Mahon to the much larger farmhouse of Binny Mathews. There are also a couple of houses that are not really cottages at all. They have been included because, rather than dwelling on the architecture of English cottages, this is a book about the decoration of their interiors. So it is that Doris Urquhart's four-storey doll's house lookalike in the middle of a small country town appears in Part Five. Although it is more cottagey than you would expect from its prim facade, the reason for its inclusion is the way it has been furnished and decorated in a look that evokes the country rather than the town, and is well suited to the modest proportions of the rooms and their lack of formal architectural detail.

Even less of a cottage is the London home of Robert Hirschhorn and John Hall. Backing onto fields when it was first built, it is nonetheless architecturally a town house. But Hall and Hirschhorn are antique dealers who specialize in the elegantly plain furniture made using local timber by local craftsmen that filled rural homes before the Industrial Revolution. Like the houses we now call cottages, the wooden settles, carved chests, grandfather clocks and Windsor chairs that are their stock and that furnish their house originally belonged to the more prosperous country dweller. But the look is pared down and simple and creates a distinctly rustic interior atmosphere despite the pavement, the yellow lines and streetlights beyond their front door.

All of the cottages featured in this book date back a hundred years or more. The oldest ones have the low ceilings and small windows typical of more humble houses from the late 17th and early 18th centuries. Their owners have found various ways to enhance the sense of space and light, whether by building new extensions, by opening rooms up into the rafters or by judicious use of colour.

The book is divided into chapters by mood rather than according to specific styles, celebrating what you might call the poetry of the cottage interior as opposed to the prose of its visual language. Unlike cottage architecture, which has arguably coalesced into a recognizable style, cottage interiors remain endlessly open to interpretation. Each home featured is as individual as its inhabitants, mirroring their tastes and preoccupations, and organized to suit their particular needs. Six are second homes, and one has been designed for rent as a holiday cottage. Five are places of work as well as homes. All are inspiring in their own way; all, as Felicia Dorothea Hemans put it, are 'smiling'.

Ros Byam Shaw

ROMANCE

THE RURAL IDYLL IS A DREAM WE WOULD LIKE
TO BELIEVE IN: A LAND OF GENTLE COWS AND
HAYRICKS, FRESH EGGS AND THATCH, THE PLACE
WHERE ALL OUR FAVOURITE CHILDREN'S STORIES
ARE SET, THE IMAGINED ANTIDOTE TO STRESS
AND THE CITY. THE COTTAGES IN THIS CHAPTER
TAP INTO THAT SENSE OF THE ROMANTIC; THEIR
FURNISHINGS AND DECORATION INSPIRED BY
NOSTALGIA. HERE ARE ROSES ROUND THE
DOOR, LOG FIRES, SLEEPY DOGS, FADED CHINTZ,
FLOWERY APRONS AND BOWLS OF FRESHLY
PICKED RASPBERRIES, AND FOR THEIR OWNERS
THE DREAM COME TRUE.

COTTAGE KITSCH

Peter Westcott's Somerset cottage is instantly loveable. Just the sight of its dear little windows, its porch draped with wisteria, its front garden packed with flowers is enough to make your mouth pucker into the sort of 'ohhh' more often reserved for fat puppies and tiny kittens. 'I had been thinking about buying a house in the country for years,' says Peter, 'but kept waiting for "something better". My mum sent me the brochure for this cottage.

The steep wooden staircase leads up from a hall behind the living room at the back of the cottage. Peter has painted its treads with a 'stair carpet' of duck egg blue.

'When I came to see it, the first thing that happened before I had even reached the front door was that two turtle doves landed at my feet. Then we met the owners, Mr and Mrs Nutkin, who were adorable, still totally in love and very sad to leave the cottage, but were getting too old to maintain the garden. Later, when we were looking round the garden, we saw a kingfisher. I thought "Oh my God, it's another sign" and I knew I had to buy it.'

That was six years ago and Peter's enthusiasm for the place has barely wavered since. His working life as head of Westcott Design Ltd is London based and 'frenetic'. 'I have a fantastic team. We do print and knitwear designs, beading, embroidery and t-shirt graphics, which we sell to the big fashion labels – everyone from Primark to Dolce & Gabbana. It's fun and it keeps me young, but it's also extremely competitive, very hard work and too much travel – four big shows a year and a lot of knocking on doors with suitcases full of samples.'

ABOVE LEFT The cottage is more than 200 hundred years old and sits at right angles to the lane that winds through the middle of the village. The garden is overlooked by a vegetable patch bordered by a stream and the Victorian gothic church next door.

The kitchen table is laid for an old-fashioned tea party, complete with china cups and plates, to celebrate Peter's birthday. Homemade sandwiches and cakes are enticingly displayed on glass and china cake stands between some of the vases of garden flowers which are dotted around every room. The curtains are vintage, as is the tablecloth with its bobble fringe.

Despite his busy schedule, Peter manages to escape frequently to the cottage with his partner Andrew Merron. Having been brought up on nearby Exmoor and attended art school in Taunton, he still has local friends. 'It feels like coming home when we turn into the drive,' he says, 'and I've tried to give the interior a quiet, old-fashioned, nostalgic atmosphere, so that being here also feels a bit like going back in time.'

The cottage sits at right angles to the road in the middle of a small village and has a large garden with lawns, borders and fruit trees, and a vegetable garden with a gate at its far end leading to the bank of a small, winding river. Rising above the flowers along one side of the garden are the gothic windows of the late-Victorian village church, making a surprisingly grand backdrop to the informal planting.

BELOW The kitchen was originally two rooms, but now runs from front to back of the cottage on the opposite side of the entrance hall from the living room and staircase hall. Peter removed ceilings to reveal the beams and laid new stone flooring.

RIGHT A wall shelf at the dining end of the kitchen holds an assortment of old china and one of several vintage soft toys that perch here and there on shelves and chairs. Peter also collects vintage pictures, some of which hang on cup hooks below.

BELOW Peter bought the 1940s chair with needlepoint upholstery on eBay, while the pair of knitted 'gonks' on the ledge above are by a friend whose company is called The Village Hall. The matchboarding, added by Peter, helps to unite the space that was once two rooms.

OVERLEAF Peter's living room.

'We do what I call a lap of honour when we first arrive,' says Peter, 'and pick a selection of anything and everything that's in flower to put in vases all round the house.'

No one knows exactly how old the cottage is, but its thick walls and small windows place it as 18th century, if not earlier. Most of the changes that Peter made to the interior were a question of removing layers of modernity. Ceilings were stripped back to reveal narrow beams, which he has painted white. Upstairs he took up all the carpets to reveal the original floorboards, which he also painted white. Downstairs he put in new stone flooring and added matchboard panelling to dado level in the kitchen. The modern kitchen units were taken out and replaced with plain painted cupboards, wooden worktops and a Belfast sink under the window. A cream Aga was tucked into the old chimney breast, which must once have housed the kitchen range.

The layout of the cottage is simple and symmetrical: a narrow hall with a living room, a separate staircase hall leading off to the left and a kitchen to the right. Peter's only

TOP Upstairs Peter retained the original floorboards, even though some were damaged, and painted them the same colour throughout. Oddly, this floor of the cottage is on two slightly different levels, one of the architectural quirks that give the place its character. The window at the top of the stairs looks over the garden to the church.

ABOVE AND ABOVE RIGHT Peter calls the bedroom at the back of the cottage the 'girls' bedroom' and has decorated it accordingly with flowery fabrics and a menagerie of animals, including a flock of china swans. All the furniture is painted in pastel shades and the bedside table is stacked with vintage children's books. The unusual 1930s butterfly mirror was bought for £16 in a local charity shop.

concession to contemporary taste was to double the size of the kitchen by taking out a partition wall that divided it from a front room opposite the living room. Up the steep, wooden staircase there are two bedrooms above the kitchen, and a third bedroom and bathroom above the living room and hall.

As for furnishings, Peter didn't want anything to look new. 'Our house in London is quite slick and sophisticated,' he says, 'but I wanted this place to be a real contrast.' Peter has been buying and selling vintage fabrics for some years. 'They are a great source of inspiration for my work,' he explains, 'but the cottage gave me another reason for keeping them,

and a way of using them.' All the curtains in the house are vintage, except for the pair in the living room in a fabric called 'Imperialis', which was designed by Peter when he worked for Designers Guild in the mid-1980s. Also made in vintage fabrics are the cushions, which are mounded on the living room sofa and neatly propped on the beds. There are old rag rugs on the floors, crocheted blankets over the backs of chairs, antique patchwork quilts on the beds and a faded floral tablecloth draped over the kitchen table.

The furniture is in the same vein, dating from the 1930s to the 1950s, much of it bought very cheaply in markets, junk shops and even charity shops. A pair of

The metal bedstead, like the
other two beds in the cottage,
was bought from a sale at
After Noah; the mattress from
The Bed Bazaar. Piled vintage
cushions, an old patchwork
quilt, a vintage eiderdown and
plaid blanket make the bed look
particularly inviting.

metal tables in the living room, for example, cost £5 each, while a 1950s chair upholstered in needlework and tucked into an alcove in the kitchen was £10. But it is the ornaments and pictures that give the cottage its distinctive look. In addition to the more tasteful collections of fabric-covered boxes and flowery teacups, there is a whole menagerie of kitsch animals, from the flock of china swans that sail across the top of a bedroom chest of drawers to the pair of

TOP LEFT The bathroom is at the back of the cottage and would once have been its fourth bedroom. Bath and basin have been panelled with painted matchboard and there is also space for a few pieces of quirky vintage furniture, such as the French metal chair and the cabinet on the windowsill for toiletries.

LEFT The cottage retains its wooden casement windows, although it is likely that the panes of glass would have been smaller when the place was first built. The facade is shrouded in greenery in the summer, including roses and wisteria.

FAR LEFT Peter's bedroom is at the front of the cottage with another metal bedstead from After Noah and more patchwork, including a Victorian bedspread and patchwork curtains. The toadstool doorstop, which Peter refers to as 'the pixie asylum', was made by Peter's friend Bubby Murr for her company The Village Hall.

LEFT Outside the front door, tucked in beside the wooden porch, there is a sheltered and sunny seating area. The rustic bench is draped with a colourful quilted throw from Pakistan, an old-fashioned plaid blanket and cushions covered in vintage floral fabrics, which Peter buys as inspiration for his work as well as to decorate the cottage.

BELOW In the front bedroom opposite Peter's, the unlined curtains made from vintage fabric are hung from simple curtain clips and a metal rail from IKEA. The pots of geraniums on the windowsill add a touch of traditional cottage charm.

painted plaster 'Bambi' lamps that flank the sofa and a variety of worn stuffed toys that catch you with their beady eyes from shelves and the corners of armchairs. Pictures include sentimental images of Jesus, Constance Spry-style bunches of flowers and various baby animals; the kind of pictures you loved as a child. 'I call it "ironic cute",' smiles Peter.

The upstairs bedroom at the back of the house is particularly teeming with wildlife – home to the swans, a china Bambi and birds, a mirror shaped like a butterfly and a doorstop in the shape of a duck. The iron bedstead is topped by a flowery patchwork and cushions. 'This is what we call the girls' bedroom,' says Peter. 'When it was finished I had my two nieces to stay. They were very young, about five and seven, and I tucked them into the bed and started reading them a Beatrix Potter story. I imagined they would think it

complete heaven. But I had only read a few pages when one of them said something along the lines of "give it a break", at which point I realized that their idea of a perfect childhood was not quite the same as my own.'

As if to complete the old-fashioned, storybook charm, it turns out that there is a ghost, and in the best of happy endings, one that is both benign and protective. 'I had a visit from a very dodgy second-hand Aga salesman when we first moved in. I didn't like the look of him at all and was convinced he was casing the joint. He was dawdling in the living room when he suddenly panicked, said he had seen "a huge face" and scarpered.' Peter made his peace with the ghost early on. 'I told her that she could have the place to herself all week, but that I was coming at weekends whether she liked it or not. And I think she does like it now.'

LEFT This large, light first-floor room was Leonard Woolf's bedroom, but is now used by Jonathan and Caroline Zoob as a sitting room. There are windows on three sides of the room, two looking through the roof of the conservatory to the gardens that stretch away towards the church behind the house, one side window and one with a view onto the quiet, leafy lane at the front. The house is 18th century and originally this space would have been divided into smaller bedrooms. Caroline and Jonathan have painted the walls and the wooden ceiling and dividing structural beams white, maximizing the room's airy feel.

RIGHT The room is now heated by a wood-burning stove and furnished with a selection of simple country furniture, mostly also painted white. The red geranium is colour-coded to match a fresh, pretty scheme of fabrics in soft reds and pinks, including the red and white checked blinds that hang at the windows.

BELOW RIGHT In the same room, a white-painted dresser serves as storage and bookshelves.

LITERARY LEGACY

In the middle of the flat fields that lie between the edge of the Sussex Downs and the sea, there is a small, rambling village of flint walls and red brick. It is a pretty place, but would be unremarkable except for the fact that it was once home to Virginia and Leonard Woolf. Down these quiet, narrow lanes drove some of the greatest minds and talents of the 20th century – T.S. Eliot, Maynard Keynes, Lytton Strachey, E.M. Forster, Roger Fry – all of whom visited the Woolfs at Monk's House, the holiday retreat that in 1940 became their permanent home.

The house dates from the late 17th century and the facade is clad in white-painted weatherboarding. At one end there is an extension, built in 1929 on the proceeds of Virginia's first successful novel, *Orlando*, and along the back of the house is a deep, lean-to conservatory. Behind this attractive, if unexceptional, village house is a garden of surprising scale and beauty, laid out by Leonard Woolf, an enthusiastic, talented gardener. Virginia loved the garden too, and chose to write in a wooden summerhouse from where she could see the Downs.

After Virginia's death in 1941, Leonard stayed in the cottage, nurturing and embellishing the gardens until he died in 1969. Today the house belongs to The National Trust, its low, brick-floored rooms still housing the painted furniture, the paintings and carefully chosen antique furniture that belonged to Virginia and Leonard. There is an eerie, almost static feel to these downstairs rooms, as if those upper-class accents and intellectual debates continue to echo in spaces where very little has happened since. But beyond and above the rooms that are on show to the public, the house now has a new life, as home to tenants Jonathan and Caroline Zoob.

ABOVE The kitchen is a long room that runs from front to back of the house. The front of the kitchen, with windows overlooking the lane, is screened from the public and is Jonathan and Caroline's private space. Curtains have been cut from an antique patchwork quilt and simply hung on a metal rail. The tea cosy is another example of antique patchwork. The wooden drawers are from an Italian grocery, and include the appropriate label 'Riz Caroline'. Caroline uses the drawers to store small kitchen items.

RIGHT A linen pelmet embroidered in a simple, old-fashioned design by Caroline hangs at the kitchen window behind the sink. Pretty, antique teacups mixed with some of Caroline's own design china hang on cup hooks next to it.

FAR RIGHT At the other end of the kitchen, a door opens into the conservatory added by Leonard Woolf so that he could indulge his passion for exotic plants. The floor retains its old terracotta tiles and the walls are painted in cream gloss. Strawberries and raspberries from the extensive vegetable garden fill bowls designed by Caroline.

Caroline tells the story of how they came to live here with an undiminished sense of wonder at their good fortune. 'We were living in London where I had just qualified as a solicitor,' she remembers. 'We had no plans to move, but we are both passionate gardeners, so when I spotted a newspaper article about the tenancy at Monk's House, it leapt off the page. We first saw the house on the most beautiful day in early June. As we came round the back and saw the garden, I stopped and said to Jonathan that I didn't think I could bear to look around if he was just humouring me, but he too had suffered a *coup de foudre*.' In retrospect, Caroline says they barely noticed the house or indeed its interior on that first visit. It was the garden that they had fallen in love with, and the idea of looking after it.

Jonathan is a pensions manager based in London, but Caroline changed direction after the move, turning a hobby into a career. Now an embroiderer and textile designer, she sells her homewares by mail order. The gentle, old-fashioned style of her designs informs the way she has decorated their rooms. 'There is a quiet simplicity about this place,' she says. 'Virginia called it "an unpretending house". I felt it needed cloudy greys, and grey-greens and lots of pale colours. But it isn't a house that likes being all white, nor is it a smart house. Vintage fabrics and old patchwork quilts thrown over chairs look right, and we found one of Virginia's armchairs in the garage and had loose covers made for it from old French linen sheets.'

Although Jonathan and Caroline use part of the kitchen, the rest of the rooms they occupy are upstairs: Leonard's bedroom is now their sitting room, their own bedroom was a spare room, Leonard's long, thin study up in the slope of the roof is still a study and the room that Leonard and Virginia used as a sitting room is Caroline's sewing room with the best views of the garden. The bathroom, installed in 1926 where Virginia would take a long morning bath reciting lines from her latest novel, is unchanged.

'There are no mod cons at Monks,' smiles Caroline. 'The plumbing is fragile to say the least. In a sense, living here you have to opt out of many of the things people take for granted – good lighting, proper central heating, access to modern technology. But I get quite cross when people ask if we feel Virginia's sad and suicidal spirit lurking in every corner. We don't. Virginia and Leonard loved this house and were very happy here. As are we.'

LEFT Caroline and Jonathan's mission was to lighten spaces that could have felt gloomy and confined such as the narrow landing that was carpeted with dark brown carpet tiles. They painted walls and woodwork white and replaced the carpet with seagrass. The stairs lead up to Leonard's study, while the living room was formerly his bedroom.

RIGHT The bathroom was installed in 1926 by the Woolfs in a room made by partitioning a bedroom and adding a window. Its fittings and layout have not changed since, but Caroline has added her own style with beautiful antique lace curtains and antique embroidered linen towels.

BELOW T.S. Eliot noted when he came to stay with the Woolfs that the bathwater was higher on one side of the bath than the other. Caroline says that this is still the case because the floor slopes hugely to one side.

FAR RIGHT Sara Mahon's cottage is about 3.6 m (12 ft) wide, which is also the width of her living room, a space that serves equally as the hall, study and dining room. When she bought the cottage, the original fireplace had been replaced with a modern one, which, she says, dominated the room in all the wrong ways. Sara opened up the old fireplace and copied its brick surround from the one in the cottage next door. The three-piece suite's diminutive proportions are perfect for the room, its rips and tears covered by vintage blankets that also make a bed for one of Sara's two lurchers, Feathers.

RIGHT Sara's table doubles as a dining and work table. The walls in this corner had been stripped of plaster by the previous owners and the stonework left bare for a faux rustic look that Sara has minimized by painting it the same colour as the rest of the room.

BELOW One of the attractions of the cottage for Sara, who has worked as a professional gardener, was the large garden to grow flowers and vegetables.

GIRL'S OWN HOME

Sara Mahon's shop in Bridport, Dorset is full of slightly old-fashioned but useful and useable things. There are tartan wool blankets, enamel storage jars, mugs decorated with spots or stripes, flowery peg bags and wooden doorstops. There are also toys of the aesthetically pleasing variety, little brooches made from scraps of old embroidery and hand-knitted Fair Isle berets, fingerless gloves and baby tank tops. Called 'Girl's Own Store', the shop transports you back to an idealized past of picnics from the boot of a Morris Minor and grandma's trifle.

Girl's Own Store is not a large shop, but the cottage of its owner would fit quite neatly into it, with space around the edges. In the middle of a short terrace, Sara says hers is the only cottage that is its original width. 'This used to be a row of six cottages,' she explains, 'but two of the pairs have been knocked together, and the one at the end has been extended. It's hard to imagine how families of ten managed to squeeze in,' she says, gesturing round her small front room.

On the main street of a Dorset village, the cottages were built in the 18th century for farm labourers. The big house next door is still a farm, while the cottage at the end nearest to the road used to be the post office. 'The post office has been in various places over the years,' says Sara 'but now it's nowhere,' referring to its recent closure.

Sara's cottage, unlike those of her neighbours, cannot be more than about 3.6 m (12 ft) across, and the front door opens straight into the living room. At the back, where there was once a lean-to scullery, there is a pocket-sized kitchen and a tiny bathroom. Wooden stairs lead up from the far corner of the living room to a front and back bedroom. It would certainly be crowded if it were home to a family of ten, but for one small woman and two slim dogs, it is just the right size.

Five years ago, when Sara bought the cottage, it seemed even smaller. 'I had been working as a live-in gardener at a big house in Sussex, and I kept coming down West for weekends and odd days away, and always looked in estate agents' windows to see if there was anything I could afford. I had already sold my London flat, so I had the money waiting in the bank, and what really attracted me to this place was not so much the cottage itself, which was pretty hideous inside, but the fact that it has a really good-sized garden.' Sarah pulls out the estate agent's particulars from a drawer to illustrate her point about the interior. Even through the distorted eye of a wide-angle lens, the living room looks cramped, dominated by a fake-stone feature fireplace and inappropriately large furniture.

LEFT The kitchen is in a lean-to at the back of the cottage, its organization an object lesson in how to make the most of limited space. The wall tiles are inexpensive standard tiles, laid in a brick pattern for added visual interest. The small Belfast sink is set into a wooden work surface with curtained cupboards beneath. The plate rack stores crockery, while the rail and hooks store utensils.

RIGHT Shallow, mounted shelves are a practical and good-looking way to store foodstuffs, some in vintage tins. The tiny table and folding chair fit neatly against the wall, providing extra work surface and a breakfast perch.

The work surface next to the cooker is a thick piece of oak that Sara used as a coffee table on breeze blocks in her last home. The 1950s wall cabinet houses more of Sara's vintage storage tins.

'Everything from the boiler to the staircase had been boxed in,' Sara says. 'There were fake arches, there was a little fake-stone nook for the video machine and there was a wine rack in the kitchen with empty space behind it. It was very easy to dismantle, as it had all been so badly made, and when I did I discovered quite a lot of extra space. When you live somewhere as small as this – "limited accommodation", as the surveyor described it – even a gap behind a wine rack is vital.'

Sara put down a slate floor in the kitchen, coir matting in the living room and pulled up the hardboard and carpet upstairs to leave the original wide pine floorboards bare. She also painted all the woodwork, including the planked kitchen ceiling. 'It had been stained dark "mahogany" brown,' she says, wrinkling her nose. 'As if a humble, little cottage like this would have had mahogany doors and ceilings.'

The kitchen is a model of how to make the most of 'limited accommodation', and of a limited budget. In a space only about 2.4 m (8 ft) square, and with two doors, one from the living room and one opening into the alley at the back, she has fitted sink, cooker, fridge, storage for food, crockery and utensils and even a table and accompanying chair. The chunky oak work surface next to the cooker was free, rescued from a kitchen that was being replaced; the 1950s wall cupboard was £80; and the white tiles are bottom of the range.

ABOVE The bathroom is downstairs next to the kitchen at the back of the house and Sara has used the same inexpensive wall tiles, again laid in a brick pattern. She kept the bath and basin that were already there and replaced the modern taps with old-fashioned ones. The vintage metal wall cupboard is an old medicine cabinet.

LEFT There are two small bedrooms upstairs. This bedroom at the back of the house is the spare bedroom and overlooks the farmyard of the farm where the labourers who lived in these cottages once worked. Sara does all her own sewing and made the Roman blind for this room using a colourful vintage fabric depicting romanticized Italian townscapes. The blind fits snugly into the deep window embrasure, leaving the windowsill free for ornaments and vases of garden flowers.

The Victorian metal cot bed in the spare bedroom is covered with an old patchwork quilt and cushions with floral vintage fabric covers made by Sara. The curtained shelf at the end of the bed provides hidden storage. The Cindy doll in the basket belonged to Sara as a child. Sara says, 'She must have real staying power to have avoided all my purges.'

Sara's bedroom is mostly filled by a large Edwardian bed but there is just space in the corner for what she calls her 'upstairs office'. Baskets provide storage for knitting materials, while the Lloyd Loom chair continues the woven theme. The curtains are vintage and the original floorboards were found intact under a layer of carpet and hardboard.

Saucepans, sieve, colander, cheese grater, whisk, ladle and more hang from hooks on metal rails, while plates, jugs, mugs and bowls are stacked on a plate rack above the sink.

Sara has maximized space, and has also minimized furniture. A neat, 1930s leather three-piece suite, bought in Spitalfields Market, is gathered around the wood-burning stove in the living room. The blankets draped over the armchairs and sofa add to the cosy feel and also, as Sara points out, cover rips and cracks in the old leather. Between the window and the front door is a very small desk, and tucked into the corner opposite the stairs is the table where Sara eats and works. The largest thing in the room is the upright piano, which Sara inherited, along with her wooden bed, from her grandmother. When not in use, the piano serves as a two-tier console table. 'It's incredibly useful for putting things on,' she says.

Sara is tidy, but claims that the shop is the secret to keeping things under control.

'If it starts to get too cluttered, I just sell something.' The two bedrooms upstairs are often temporary home to things waiting to go into the shop – vintage toys that she is saving for Christmas or cushions she has made from vintage fabrics. Sometimes she decides to keep something that hasn't sold, like the felt picture of fruit hanging in her bedroom. 'The more I looked at it, the more I liked it, so I brought it home.'

The garden is separate from the cottage, up a cinder path between the hedges and fences of her neighbours' gardens. Sara's occupies the end plot and seems enormous compared to the cottage it belongs to. There are two lawns, fruit trees, deep borders, a vegetable patch, a shed and a fully-furnished summerhouse, complete with gas rings and a kettle, armchairs, blankets, cushions and rugs. 'In summer I come up here for the day with the dogs – it's a bit like a holiday home,' she laughs. And somewhere else to put things that she doesn't want to sell.

BELOW LEFT The gardens belonging to the terrace of cottages occupy a separate plot of land reached up a cinder path. Sara's is the largest, but also the furthest from the cottage, so she has turned the old wooden summerhouse into a miniature home from home.

BELOW RIGHT Inside the summer-house there is a camp bed and also a kitchenette, complete with a gas camping stove so that Sara can take a break from gardening to have a cup of tea without having to go back to the cottage.

ROMANCE
finishing touches

• FLOWERS A jug of fresh garden flowers on the table and a row of geraniums on the windowsill are cottage essentials. One of the first things Peter Westcott does on arrival at his Somerset cottage is what he calls a 'lap of honour' of the garden to pick flowers, which he puts in jugs, mugs, bottles and vases in every room of the house. Sometimes he mixes them with common wildflowers like Queen Anne's lace or foxgloves from the hedgerows – the more blousy and informal the arrangements, the better. Even in winter there is always something green you can find to brighten a room; perhaps a bunch of glossy ivy or feathery branches of mimosa.

• MORE FLOWERS For full-on cottage romance, bring the garden indoors in every other way you can think of – flowery fabrics, flowery china, flowery wallpaper and paintings of flowers. Layer them up like Peter Westcott has in his 'girls' bedroom' and make rooms into flowery bowers.

• NOSTALGIA This is a potent element of romance. Find things in junk shops and antiques markets that remind you of your childhood or your grandparents' houses. Sara Mahon's cottage is like stepping into an Enid Blyton story – all baskets of apples, Fair Isle mittens and tartan picnic blankets; Peter Westcott piles on the nostalgia with children's books from the '40s and '50s, which he places invitingly on bedside tables; Caroline Zoob uses faded florals for cushions and upholstery.

• VINTAGE Bring nostalgia to the kitchen without compromising practicality by using vintage tins for storage, as Sara Mahon does.

• STITCHING Rediscover old-fashioned skills such as knitting, embroidery and crochet, and make yourself a tea cosy or a tray cloth. Even a novice can stitch squares to make patchwork; a traditional form of recycling and a reasonably foolproof sewing project, as long as you remember only to mix fabrics of similar weights and fibres. Using squares of heavy upholstery cotton with a light dress fabric will encourage the weaker fabric to tear. Peter Westcott has patchwork bedroom curtains and Caroline Zoob uses old patchwork quilts as throws to cover chairs and sofas.

• PAINT A coat of paint can transform an inoffensive but nondescript item of furniture into something as pretty and desirable as the dresser bookcase in Caroline Zoob's living room. Cheap modern pine is instantly improved with a few layers of a favourite colour. Convincing 'distressing' to give an appearance of wear and tear is a fine art. In my own experience, not bothering with undercoat and generally making a bad job of it has much the same effect.

• CURTAINS While on the subject of cutting corners, unlined curtains have an airy, impromptu feel and because they are light can be hung on a simple wire from curtain clips, as in Peter Westcott's bedrooms. And what could be more romantic than being woken by the first rays of dawn?

'*Ah! Yet, ere I descend to the grave,*
May I a small house and a large garden have!
And a few friends, and many books, both true,
Both wise, and both delightful too.'

ABRAHAM COWLEY (1618–1667)

CHARACTER

WHAT IS IT THAT GIVES A HOUSE CHARACTER?
PARTLY IT RESIDES IN THE FABRIC OF BUILDINGS
DATING BACK TO A TIME WHEN ARCHITECTURE
WAS A CRAFT RATHER THAN AN ART, WHEN
MATERIALS WERE LOCAL AND STYLES WERE
VERNACULAR. BUT WE HAVE ALL SEEN TIMBER-
FRAMED CHARM AND PICTURE-BOOK THATCH
RESTORED BEYOND REDEMPTION; EVERY WALL
SANITIZED WITH NEW PLASTER, EVERY WINDOW
GLEAMING WITH GINGER TIMBER AND MODERN
GLASS. ALL THE OWNERS IN THIS CHAPTER HAVE
LEFT THEIR MARK ON THE OLD BONES OF THEIR
COTTAGES, BUT DONE IT SO GENTLY THAT THEY
HAVE ADDED ANOTHER LAYER TO THEIR
ATMOSPHERE, NOT STRIPPED IT AWAY.

WARM WELCOME

Jane Moran's mother moved into a small, isolated cottage on the edge of a wooded common in Sussex, with no driving licence, a daughter at boarding school and a husband in a sanatorium recovering from tuberculosis. 'I think my father was expecting her to find some nice, convenient little town house near where he was staying, but my mother walked through the door of this cottage and immediately felt at home. They had been living in India where my father was a tea planter,' Jane continues, 'and had arrived back in England with nothing. The cottage was for sale fully furnished right down to the washing-up bowl because the owner was a writer who lived in Spain.'

FAR LEFT The lower roof line at the far end of the cottage marks the extension built by Jane Moran and Tom Eden, which is now their kitchen downstairs and their grown-up daughter Maud's bedroom above. The older part of the cottage in the foreground is built from local materials, timber-framed with rubble infill, and was originally two cottages. It is hard to date the building accurately. It appears on the census of 1840, but was probably built in the previous century.

BELOW LEFT When Jane's mother lived here, the room that is now the entrance hall was the kitchen. The pair of antique hall chairs was painted this vibrant shade of orange by Tom's father, antique dealer Robin Eden, and decorated with his own initial and that of his wife. The gorgeous cocktail of colours in this room shows that Jane has inherited what she calls her mother's 'wonderful eye for colour'.

RIGHT A steep ladder staircase rises from the same room. Slotted beneath it is one of the pieces of furniture Jane's mother bought with the cottage, a ship's piano that has one octave less than a conventional piano.

Jane's mother stayed in the cottage she loved for the rest of her life. After she died, Jane's father stayed on. 'He was tall, and the ceilings are terribly low, and I think he rather longed to pull it down and build a bungalow,' she smiles. 'But he didn't. It became completely shambolic, and he filled the field with old cars, scattered the place with bits of useful wire and batteries and kept chickens in a battered Bentley.'

Jane evokes a delightfully eccentric picture of her father in his latter years, a white-haired old man, 'wild and handsome', wearing customized clothes including cut-off trousers with hand-sewn elastic around the bottoms for playing golf. In 1991 he moved out and Jane, her husband Tom Eden and their two children, Maud aged ten and William aged seven, plus a temporarily homeless friend, a large dog and two cats, all moved in. 'So there we were,' says Jane, 'in this tiny, tiny cottage, with two bedrooms upstairs and three rooms downstairs. I think if anyone from the council had come to inspect it they would have been horrified and had it classified as a slum.'

Many things have changed since those early days. The cottage has almost doubled in size with an extension

containing a large kitchen downstairs and a third bedroom upstairs. The cottages next door have been smartened up and are now occupied, and the gypsies, who used to camp close by, making birch brooms and gathering moss to sell at the flower market, and holly and mistletoe for Christmas, have left the common to settle in the village. 'I think it still has the same atmosphere,' Jane comments thoughtfully. 'It may not be beautiful, but it is very, very welcoming and warm, which is probably why we have never left. A good friend of mine says it feels like a holiday house because the doors are always open and you never have to worry about treading mud on pristine carpet or breaking something.'

Jane is right about the atmosphere, but not about the beauty. The first room you enter seems to glow,

LEFT The kitchen is the largest room in the cottage, built as an extension in 1991 and floored with terracotta tiles to match those in the entrance hall. In addition to the small, round table set for tea, there is a large kitchen table big enough to accommodate family and friends. Aside from this cupboard set into the wall, there are no fitted cupboards. Open shelving displays a mix of new and antique crockery, most of it in constant use, and antique chests of drawers provide further storage.

TOP RIGHT An antique lustre jug, repainted as a wedding present for Tom and Jane's wedding, sits on a top shelf next to more recent spongeware mugs decorated with the names of their children.

BOTTOM RIGHT The end wall of the original cottage, which has been painted but not plastered, is behind the Rayburn. The kitchen is on a lower level than the rest of the cottage, as the land slopes away, and three steps lead up to the inner hall, beyond which is the living room.

with buttercup yellow walls, a pair of spoon-back hall chairs painted a rich orange and two contemporary paintings on the wall, one with a background the same colour as the chairs, the other vibrant with emerald greens, purple and yellow. A chest of drawers is draped with a piece of old chintz dotted with orange flowers and there is a brightly coloured tin trunk sitting on top. The effect is like stepping into a tropical garden.

When Jane's mother lived here, this room was the kitchen. With the luxury of extra space, it has become the entrance hall,

from which rises a wooden staircase as steep as a stepladder, leaving just enough space beneath for a ship's piano, which has one octave less than a normal piano. As an introduction, this room encapsulates all that makes the cottage so attractive. The modern paintings are by friends and reflect Jane's interest in contemporary art and her work running educational workshops and tours at the Pallant House Gallery in Chichester. Trained as a textile designer, she has a passion for fabrics. The piece of chintz on the chest is just one sample of a collection of antique and

ABOVE A still life of glasses, plates, decanters, a papier mâché tray and a lamp with a shade covered in William Morris paper is caught by the light from a glazed door that leads out from the inner hall into the garden where Jane has a studio.

RIGHT When the house was two cottages, this room would have been the main living room of one of them. Now it serves as an inner hall, an axis between the living room that opens off it to the left, the kitchen that opens off it to the right and the entrance hall. The pretty pair of early Victorian rosewood chairs came with the house when Jane's mother bought it fully furnished. Jane painted the floor in a geometric pattern to imitate tiles 'because we couldn't afford anything else'.

FAR RIGHT Next to the original fireplace are steps down into the new kitchen. The walls are lime-washed the blue of a summer sky.

LEFT Hanging above the fireplace in the living room is a cartoon of foxes dressed as huntsmen. 'It's a terrible thing,' laughs Jane, 'but as a child growing up in India, it was my idea of what England was like.' The sofa is wearing its summer cover of striped cotton, and an old ottoman, covered with a small kilim, makes a fine coffee table and footstool.

RIGHT The sofa on the other side of the fireplace is draped in a Victorian paisley shawl from Jane's collection of antique textiles. Shelves in the alcove hold books and early Delft plates, all broken, which Jane says she prefers 'so I don't have to worry about them'. Jane stripped the wall behind the sofa and then decided she liked the result too much to paint over it.

BELOW The corner cupboard in the same room was a 'horrible, horrible colour'. Jane took the top layer off and started rubbing it down then, like the walls, decided to leave it at that.

vintage pieces she keeps for inspiration neatly folded in the drawers beneath. The antique hall chairs were painted in this unlikely, brilliant shade by Jane's father-in-law, the influential antique dealer Robin Eden. The ship's piano came with the house.

The same mix of inherited antiques, original furnishings and things collected by Jane and by Tom, who is a coin and medal expert, fills the rest of the house. The large kitchen has wall shelves stacked with china, some old, some new, some in constant use, some purely decorative. Next to the kitchen is an inner hall with a floor painted by Jane to imitate black and white tiles, and a pair of pretty rosewood chairs, which, like the piano, were bought with the house. From here you enter the living room, which has sofas facing one another on either side of a wide brick fireplace. The long room that

leads off this room is used as a spare bedroom where fortunate guests sleep in a ship's bunk once belonging to the Captain of a German ship, a piece of nautical history purchased by Robin Eden along with another bunk in which the Kaiser slept.

Just as the contents of the house have come from various sources, so the decoration has evolved over the years. 'Or not,' says Jane. 'We have never made any really determined effort to do up the interior. In fact, most of it is pure accident. In the living room, for example, I started stripping the walls and then I rather liked the effect of the layers of paint and old plaster, so I left them. I did the same on the landing upstairs and found that gorgeous pink.' In the living room is a corner cupboard with dark, mottled paintwork like imitation tortoiseshell. Just like the walls, she started stripping it and then decided to stop. She calls it another accident, but that is to deny the skill it takes to recognize when enough is better than completion, imperfection more satisfying than an immaculate finish.

The house remains a work in progress. They may decide to paint the beams in the living room and Jane would like to decorate the bathroom with patterned wallpaper to look like a room in a favourite engraving by Ravilious. For a long time she has been deliberating on whether or not to remove the print over the living room fireplace, an Edwardian cartoon of foxes dressed in hunting pink and eating boiled eggs at a tea table. 'It's really a terrible thing,' Jane laughs, 'but it's one of the few items I have from my childhood in India. It used to belong to an uncle who lived on a very remote tea plantation. As a child it completely summed up my idea of what England was like.' It's hard not secretly to hope that it stays where it is.

LEFT At the top of the steep staircase is a room forming a generous landing between the main bedroom to the left and William's bedroom to the right. Here there are books, an old doll's house and a small gathering of soft toys sitting on an antique trunk covered in tapestry. Jane discovered the pink paint under later paper.

ABOVE A Victorian brass bedstead almost fills the main bedroom, which has a low doorway and a ceiling sloping up into the eaves. Anyone taller than 1.5 m (5 ft) needs to remember to duck. Jane's wardrobe is a curtained alcove in the wall at the foot of the bed. Aside from the carpet, the room is as simply furnished as it might have been a hundred years ago.

RIGHT The bathroom is above the entrance hall; a legacy from the days when the kitchen Rayburn also heated the water. A door at the end of the bath opens into Maud's bedroom. Jane plans to wallpaper this room in imitation of an engraving by Ravilious.

LEFT The chimneys of the one-storey cottage can just be seen projecting above some of the topiary that gives Charlotte Molesworth's garden the air of a magical kingdom. As well as birds and urns, there are clipped green spirals, balls, wedding cakes and even a topiary dog.

BELOW LEFT The front door opens straight into the kitchen. The teak screen wall, once part of a wardrobe made in India for Donald Molesworth's father, provides hanging space for coats. The treacle-coloured kitchen sink is antique stone-glazed pottery.

RIGHT Looking through the kitchen from the front door there is a view into the living room, which is the largest room in the cottage and referred to as 'the yellow room'. Before the bedroom extension was built, this room was divided into three rooms including a bathroom. The kitchen feels spacious thanks to the ceiling that extends up into the rafters. The enamelled plaque above the Rayburn started life as an old washing machine top and was swapped for one of Charlotte's linocuts. The double doors leading into 'the yellow room' were rescued from a bonfire.

GROWING BEAUTY

Some people have such a pervasive visual knack that even their rubbish is beautiful. Artist and garden designer Charlotte Molesworth and her husband Donald, who is also a gardener, have a junk heap at the edge of their garden so picturesque that it looks as though it has been designed. Artfully piled and decoratively displayed are iron railings, a register grate, a rusting trunk and the riveted bottom of a water tank. In another part of the garden there is a temporarily redundant chicken run where broken Victorian plates are arranged on decrepit wooden shelves, and a pair of discarded leather boots has grown a gorgeous blanket of thick, green moss.

LEFT When the ceiling in the kitchen came down and they decided not to replace it, Charlotte painted the walls above the yellow matchboarding with pale green and white oak leaves on a sky blue background using her own mix of whiting, size and powder colour. The corner cupboard was made around a salvaged door and decorated with Charlotte's linocuts.

BELOW LEFT The small window next to the double doors that open into the kitchen from 'the yellow room' once lit a bathroom when this room was previously divided into three. When the room was opened out, the floor was lowered to give a more comfortable ceiling height than the previous scant 2 m (7 ft). The old bricks used as flooring were found in the garden.

The boots and the railings might be happy accidents, but the rest of Charlotte and Donald's garden has a more deliberate, if equally whimsical beauty. Their cottage is on the edge of a Kent village that stretches along a quiet, straight road. To find it, you turn off and skirt the churchyard. The lane becomes a track and, as you leave the church behind you, comes to a halt at the top of their garden path. Two tall, tapered box hedges with box balls sticking out of their tops like giant, leafy lollipops edge the wavy brick paving that leads to their front door.

The cottage itself is low and so modest in scale that it seems to have sunk into its surrounding greenery. Ten acres of land enclose it, including a field at the front where their two donkeys graze and two large fields at the back where there are beehives and an old stable. The rest of the land is garden, including an extensive, productive vegetable garden and a polytunnel. There are also various outbuildings and a large, old barn, one end of which is Charlotte's studio where she paints and works on her distinctive linocuts, when not too busy working on her own and other people's gardens.

Charlotte's speciality is topiary and one of the first things she and Donald planted when they bought the cottage more than 20 years ago were rows of yew, hornbeam, beech and holly seedlings. In maturity these have been clipped to form fat hedges with undulating tops, from which sprout the outlines of birds, balls, cones, wedding cakes, spirals and a dog. Looking across the garden, their layered silhouettes appear one behind the other like scenery flats for some fantastical ballet.

Both cottage and garden were in a sorry state when Charlotte and Donald moved in on Christmas Eve with 'one light bulb and an outside lavatory'. The cottage is single storey, built of red brick, with a roof of faded terracotta Kentish peg tiles. It probably dates from the 18th century and housed the farmer who served the estate. Inside were low ceilings, small rooms and small windows to match. 'A family with four children lived here before we did,' says Charlotte, whistling at the thought. 'It must have been very cramped.'

Seven years ago they built an extension, now their bedroom, roofed in old tiles and clad in weatherboarding. This simple addition allowed them to transform the interior of the cottage by taking down internal walls and making the space that had once been bathroom, bedroom and small living room into a single living and dining room. At the same time they lowered the floor by about 15 cm (6 in), replacing the boards with bricks they excavated from the garden. Having already taken down the kitchen ceiling, thus opening the space into the rafters, they transformed the cramped accommodation to make a series of larger rooms that would be unrecognizable to former occupants.

With doors and windows open, even on days when less hardy people would be turning up the central heating, the house feels as much part of the garden as the hedges that frame it. And just as there is something of the fairytale about the winding paths, the sunken pond,

ABOVE The table in 'the yellow room' was inherited from Donald's father and is made of the same Indian teak as the giant wardrobe, which became bed, office drawers, coat-hanging area and wardrobe doors. Kentish hops provide a decorative fringing along the beams and homegrown gourds join the display of china on the painted dresser. The colourful picture of a farmyard is a ply woodcut by artist friend Andrew Mockett. Molo watches proceedings from the safety of his basket.

the clipped creatures and green geometry outside, the interior has a rustic richness and romance that inspires the same kind of fascination as a gloriously painted and fitted gypsy caravan.

Charlotte worked as an art teacher at Benenden School for 20 years before deciding to devote more of her time to gardens, and the walls of every room in her house are tessellated with pictures. Art runs in her blood, as does gardening, and in the larger of the living rooms which they call 'the yellow room' there are pictures by Charlotte, by her mother and by her grandmother hanging next to one another like a family tree of artistic styles. Charlotte's is a vibrant study of chickens, that of her mother a delicate watercolour of a slightly dishevelled blackbird and her grandmother's is a formal oil painting of her daughter, Charlotte's mother, dressed in Elizabethan costume.

Many of the walls have also been painted with patterns and motifs by Charlotte. 'I couldn't bear to use emulsion,' she says. Instead, she has painted directly onto the old plaster using a mix of whiting, size and powder paint; white oak leaves on a sky blue background on the walls above the old ceiling level of the kitchen and a tracery of leaves that wind their way behind the pictures in the cosy 'front room' that leads off the kitchen.

Furnishings are plain, country pieces: a painted dresser, a pale teak table and a sofa in the yellow room, a smaller table, where they always eat breakfast, and a group of armchairs in the front room. But you don't really notice the furniture because there are so many other things to attract the eye. Competing for attention with the pictures and patterns on the walls are shelves, windowsills and mantelpieces bustling with pieces of old china, from great big blue and white meat plates to little birds, jugs, mugs, cups and saucers, a pelican tureen, pairs of lions, shoes, cows and people.

The bedroom is the least-crowded room with the most natural light. Pretty gothic windows overlook either the topiary or a fig tree decked with bright green fruit. Here there are fewer pictures on the

LEFT Charlotte Molesworth describes herself as 'an open window person' and she is certainly not someone who relies on central heating. This small wood-burning stove warms 'the yellow room' and, when lit, always has a kettle sitting on its top that eventually boils. Charlotte painted the walls herself with a large paisley design.

ABOVE To the left of the sofa is the door leading to the bedroom extension. Above the sofa a shelf is crammed with eccentric china, including a pelican tureen given to Charlotte as a leaving present from the people she worked with painting scenery at the Royal Opera House. The Elizabethan lady is a portrait of Charlotte's mother painted by her grandmother.

walls, fewer ornaments on the surfaces and a majestically simple four-poster bed carved from wood the colour of honey. This is just one of several pieces in the house made from a single, enormous teak wardrobe, which belonged to Donald's father who lived in India. As well as the bed, by joiner Andrew Shelton, there are panelled doors for the fitted wardrobes, drawers that Charlotte uses for filing in her tiny study and a wooden screen next to the front door on which they hang coats. 'It was a huge piece of furniture,' nods Charlotte, 'you really could have lived in that wardrobe.'

OVERLEAF Charlotte's front room.

ABOVE The bathroom was originally the larder and has a spartan, ancient feel with its beams and flaking limewash. Before they built their bedroom extension, this space was used as storage for Charlotte's extensive wardrobe of beautiful and exotic clothing, some dating back to her art school days, much of it found in charity shops. The folding plank door at the far end opens into Charlotte's tiny study area, from where a door on the right opens into the 'front room'.

RIGHT Charlotte and Donald's bedroom is a new extension with gothic arched windows on two sides, one overlooking a wonderland of topiary, the other into the midst of a very productive fig tree. The bed was made for them from Donald's father's giant Indian teak wardrobe by joiner Andrew Shelton. Hanging on the wardrobe doors, which were made from the same giant wardrobe, is a gorgeous paisley coat that Charlotte swapped for one of her paintings.

In a house full of oddity, whether the collection of carved elephants in Donald's study, or the shallow stone-glazed kitchen sink the colour of dark treacle, perhaps the most surprising room of all is the bathroom. Entering it from Donald's study, you push open a section of wooden wall so slim that it would surely exclude a significant chunk of the population. Stepping down, you find yourself in a narrow brick-floored space, its beams and crumbly plaster crusted with old white limewash, as if dusted with snow. A carved wooden squirrel crouches at the back of the capacious wooden lavatory seat, the enamel bath is naked from its rim down and the basin is propped rather than fitted.

This small, plain room feels like the oldest, most atmospheric bathroom you'll ever get to use. There is no lock, just a cloth stuffed in at the top to keep the door shut, and at the other end another door made from hinged planks to Charlotte's study, which in turn opens into the front room leading into the kitchen. As a child, you might be tempted to go round and round, from the kitchen, through the bathroom, back through the dining room and into the kitchen again.

Contrary to appearance, the bathroom is relatively new, installed at the same time the bedroom extension was built, using the room that used to be the larder. Charlotte's study, also part of that larder, has original deal shelving, and the bathroom retains the ceiling bracket that supported the plank on which cheeses were stored. It's a brilliant, slightly eccentric use of space. And, like so many aspects of this intriguing house and garden, unaffectedly original.

FAR LEFT Gerry Peachey can make anything in wood – from medieval cupboards to curved bath surrounds – but his speciality is shepherd's huts, which he constructs using only reclaimed materials.

ABOVE RIGHT The cottage was built circa 1800 for the head gardener of the nearby estate. Today it is surrounded by more modern buildings, but once you have closed the garden gate behind you and stepped into the lush front garden where chickens roam freely, you might as well be down a country lane surrounded by fields.

LEFT Gerry added the conservatory at the side of the cottage using salvaged windows and doors built against the stone wall that borders the garden. The mosaic-fronted cabinet came from a French convent.

RIGHT The kitchen is an extension and is furnished just as interestingly as the rest of the cottage. Gerry's 'cabinet of curiosities' on the back wall was constructed around glazed 18th-century doors. Its contents include things that belonged to his relatives. The two apparently antique cabinets were both made by Gerry, the floor cupboard using wood from a neighbour's gate.

CARVING HISTORY

When Gerry Peachey was seven his father gave him an upright piano. 'He told me to take it apart,' says Gerry. 'He knew it would keep me quiet for a long time. Do you know how well a piano is made – the joints, the strength, the complexity? It took me weeks and weeks and was the best lesson I ever had.' The piano remained in pieces, but Gerry has since more than compensated for this early work of destruction. As a teenager he was apprenticed as a joiner and carpenter to the firm that restored Highgrove House. He can make anything in wood; from staircases to gothic cupboards and shepherd's huts, the building of which using reclaimed materials is his current business.

Bar the walls and the roof, he as good as made his own cottage. 'It was derelict when I bought it,' he says. 'It hadn't been lived in for some time, there were mushrooms growing indoors and the windows were boarded up. The day I collected the keys and drove over to take possession, the first thing I saw was a fire engine and smoke. I couldn't face it and just kept driving.' When he had gathered the courage to return, he found there had been a fire in an outhouse and, just to be on the safe side, the firemen had doused the interior. His new home was not only derelict but completely sodden.

Fortunately, Gerry had somewhere else to live while he set to work making the cottage habitable. The building dates from about 1800 and was the head gardener's cottage for the nearby estate. Once it must have been surrounded by fields and trees, but today its pretty facade of pale Cotswold stone, with its roof of uneven stone slates, is an oasis of period charm, with a housing association car park on two sides and a bungalow next door. The house is shielded from the road by a deep and bushy front garden entered through a rickety wooden gate. Close the gate behind you and car parks and

bungalows are instantly forgotten. There are chickens in a run with a little tin house to roost in, there are bunches of grapes festooned across a downstairs window and there is a pond.

Gerry bought the cottage in the early 1990s. Then, nearly ten years ago, he met Fran Price and they now have two children, Louis and Fred. By the time Fran moved in, Gerry had built an extension on one side of the two-up, two-down cottage housing a kitchen and utility room downstairs and a bathroom above. But he had only just put in central heating. 'He put it in for me, and I thought it was very romantic,' Fran smiles. There have been various changes since: a crazy pattern of zebra

RIGHT The cottage has two living rooms to the right and left of the front door. The left-hand living room pictured on this page, which is known as 'the green room' in honour of its carpet, leads into the kitchen. Gerry made the stick-back chair using turkey oak from a silage pit for its seat. Above hangs 'the pizza box', an experiment in colour painted on a cardboard lid by Fran, while the table lamp is an early example of Gerry's woodturning.

FAR LEFT Furnishings that have not been made from scratch by Gerry have been rescued or restored by him. This 18th-century walnut chest of drawers had been ruined with inexplicable layers of gloss black paint. Gerry painstakingly stripped it and managed to revive its patina. The painting above it is a 19th-century copy of a 17th-century still life that Gerry was given in lieu of payment for making two wardrobes. The 1930s plaster head was bought from an Irish antique dealer.

LEFT Beneath the window in 'the green room' is a large, squashy sofa and, next to it, an unusual 17th-century oak side table that Gerry says 'has been in the family for ages'. The carved female figure was passed down from Gerry's grandfather, who was head groom to various grand households and who frequently acquired 'cast-offs' from them. The oil painting of a boy in a tricorn hat was found by Gerry's mother in her attic.

BELOW The front door of the cottage leads straight into the room known as 'the big room' which occupies the right-hand side of the cottage. Until he met Fran and installed central heating, Gerry relied on heat from the open fires. Hanging to the right of the fireplace is a carved and gessoed 16th-century caryatid, which Gerry says 'is probably my favourite thing'.

RIGHT Opposite the fireplace is a late 17th-century chest, complete with its original handles, given to Gerry as a present by an antique restorer. He had converted the chest to make a stereo cabinet, an act of commercial vandalism of which he subsequently repented and that he hoped Gerry would reverse. The standard lamp has a shade embellished with antique lace.

stripes on the landing floor painted by Gerry while Fran was in labour, a third bedroom created in the roof space, a patchwork conservatory and a corner of extra kitchen worktop made from the marble top of a coffee table belonging to Fran's parents. At the back of the house is a lean-to workshop, which probably once housed a horse and trap. Gerry hasn't given either of his sons a piano yet, but he does let them use some of his tools. Aged seven, Louis

has already made a shoe rack, which is in use in the entrance lobby, and a 'treasure box' with leather hinges.

Although the house is not large, a tour of its interior takes a long time, as there are interesting stories attached to so many of its features and contents. What Gerry lacked in funds he made up for with craftsmanship and ingenuity. Take the kitchen, which is floored in dark glazed bricks salvaged from the larger of the two downstairs living rooms. Kitchen

The mantelpiece is home to a charmingly quirky group of objects, including a landscape painting entitled 'Cedar Walk, Butleigh', which was a present to Gerry from a friend, a walnut love spoon carved by Gerry following a Welsh tradition as a Valentine present for Fran, an African fertility carving picked up by Fran on her travels and a toy wooden rabbit bought for Louis at a Christmas market.

BELOW In a corner of the main bedroom the family cat sleeps on an 18th-century ladder-back chair given to Gerry by an antique dealer because it only had three legs. Above it hangs a framed box of Victorian specimen butterflies from a hotel in Aviemore. The curtain is a piece of antique silk patterned with birds bought from an antique textile shop in Bath. Suspended from two hooks at night and detached in the morning, this is as simple a curtain treatment as you could get.

RIGHT The view through the bathroom door and along the landing shows the wild zebra stripe design that Gerry painted as 'displacement activity' while Fran was in the first throws of labour. Doors on the right lead into the two first-floor bedrooms, and the high-level window in the wall is a salvaged 18th-century leaded fanlight from over a door. The wooden staircase winds up to two attic rooms.

cupboards, wooden work surfaces and draining board were all made by Gerry. 'The whole thing cost £70, and £30 of that was the taps,' he says proudly. On the back wall is a glazed cupboard, constructed around a pair of 18th-century doors. Fran calls it 'Gerry's cabinet of curiosities' and warns that if you open it everything will fall out. Gerry enumerates its contents: a stirrup presented by Queen Mary to his father who kept livery stables, his great-grandfather's Sunday cider mug, china flowers found in a box of rubbish, a lime wood cherub and his parents' corkscrews. 'I never paid for one thing in that cupboard,' he says. 'But everything in it represents some aspect of my life; friends, people I've met, trips to Spain and America.'

On another wall is a gothic cupboard, its carved wooden tracery backed by wire netting, its interior painted pea green. 'That was what I used to call a long weekend job,' Gerry comments. 'Back in my bachelor days I used to start making something on a Friday night, and if I hadn't finished it by Sunday evening, that would be the end of it.' The cupboard beneath, which looks medieval, was made by Gerry using wood from a neighbour's gate.

The kitchen leads into the room they call 'the green room' in honour of the carpet. Here there is a piece of ancient-looking furniture also made by Gerry, this time using wood that was the flooring of a cattle truck. 'It had that gnarled look that suggested an early design,' he explains. The stick-back chair, also by Gerry, has a Turkey oak seat ready patinated by cattle urine, having been used to wall a silage pit. In the same room, the golden, figured walnut of the 18th-century chest was carefully disinterred by Gerry from beneath several layers of gloss black paint.

Gerry looks around the room. 'I don't think there's much in here I had to pay for either,' he announces. The painting above the chest, a 19th-century copy of a 17th-century Dutch flower painting, was bartered for two wardrobes he made, and the copy of a Cézanne over the fireplace was 'a two-hour job – just so I could hang something on the wall' with a B&Q frame antiqued using black gesso. A third painting, a study in saturated colour with the intensity of a Rothko, is known as 'the pizza box' and was 'an experiment' painted on a cardboard lid by Fran.

BELOW Gerry painted the window wall in the main bedroom in a pattern copied from a tiny photograph in a magazine of a piece of 17th-century embossed and gilded leather wall hanging. He found the bed in a farmer's shed and the farmer was happy to let Gerry have it, as his mother-in-law had died in it. The 17th-century oak chest came from an American art dealer client in part payment for work. The dome of birds is Victorian.

LEFT Gerry kept the bath, but customized it by sawing off one of its corners with an angle grinder and panelling it in curved wood. The timber surrounding the bath and the washbasin is teak salvaged from a school science laboratory. The mirror over the basin was made by Gerry from the zinc frame of a French chateau dormer window. The Venetian blind is from B&Q and the fabric over it is one of many samples found by Fran on a skip outside an architect's office when she worked for Mencap in Swansea.

RIGHT AND BELOW When the second of their two sons was born, Gerry and Fran decided they needed extra space and converted the attic into two rooms that are lit by a reclaimed cast-iron skylight window. The dividing wall is made from deal boards from a disintegrating shepherd's hut, which in turn had been made from old packing cases from an American RAF base.

Upstairs there are more Gerry-built marvels, including a painted, serpentine-front chest of drawers, built around three 18th-century drawers. The drawers still have their original hand-blocked blue paper lining. 'Delicious,' says Gerry. And then there is the bed, which looks like a design by Voysey, and the bath that is enclosed in elegantly curved panelling. 'It was square,' Gerry explains, 'but I cut the corner off and boxed it in with MDF.' One wall in the bathroom is painted by Gerry in a design copied from Charleston, while the pattern that covers the window wall in the main bedroom was inspired by a photograph of 17th-century gilded leather from Cordoba.

Downstairs we find something that Gerry did not rescue from a bonfire, 'stumble across', swap or make. Hanging by the fireplace in the room they ambitiously call 'the big room' is a carved and gessoed caryatid, probably 16th century. 'I actually had to pay for that,' Gerry admits. 'But it is one of my favourite things.'

WILLOW PATTERN

The downstairs cloakroom of Malcolm and Anna Seal's Dorset cottage is difficult to leave. This is not because the lock sticks, but because it is packed full of things that demand inspection. Like the strange crook-shaped brush that shares a pot behind the loo with a wooden sword and a walking stick topped by a dangerously hooked bird's beak. Or the sepia photograph of two Edwardian gentlemen on bicycles. Or the metal shield tucked behind the pipe to the wall-mounted cistern, from which also hang an army water bottle, some old-fashioned keys, a vintage alarm clock, a pair of heavy workman's boots and rowlocks from a wooden boat. Then there are the shelves, high ones on one side for storing shoes and low ones opposite piled with Observer's books of eggs, fishes, insects and trees.

LEFT The cottage is built on the side of a hill on what Malcolm Seal thinks was a medieval strip lynchet, or farmed terrace, and the small sitting room has far-reaching views across the fields of a wide Dorset valley. Furnishings and fabrics are all second-hand, bought cheaply at markets or in junk shops, and the room is heated by a wood-burning stove. 'The most expensive things in the house,' says Malcolm, 'are the lampshades by Lush Designs, and even those were all seconds.'

ABOVE The two strands of Malcolm Seal's career, as basket-maker and as garden designer, come together in his own cottage garden, which is as productive as it is pretty. Woven cone plant supports rise up from the vegetable patch waiting to be climbed all over, while closer to the cottage a rose is tied in a graceful curve.

BELOW Malcolm's workshop where he stores and prepares the willow for his baskets is in one of the buildings of an Edwardian model farm just down the lane from his cottage. As well as baskets of all shapes and sizes, Malcolm makes garden furniture, and has even created a willow boat.

Despite its cramped dimensions, this humble room seems to contain enough interesting artefacts to fill a small museum, one particularly devoted to boys and their enthusiasms. Appropriately enough, it is known as 'the boys' loo' in honour of Alf (Alfred) and Ned (Edwin), Malcolm and Anna's sons who are at the primary school down the road, where Anna works as a teacher.

The rest of the house is no less interesting. Like Gerry Peachy's cottage, it was built as accommodation for the head gardener of a large estate. Architecturally it is plain enough: red brick with small-paned casement windows. A front door, never used, leads into a tiny staircase hall, with a small living room to the right, a larger living room ahead and a small kitchen leading off it, with the cloakroom and a larder behind, next to the back door. Upstairs are three bedrooms and a bathroom. The accommodation is plain and workmanlike, but the view is ravishing and the contents of every room, are so intriguing that, again as in Gerry Peachy's house, a guided

tour can take a whole afternoon.

Malcolm Seal has two interwoven threads to his career: gardens and baskets. He both makes baskets and teaches basket-making, work for which he grows his own willow, and he advises on gardens and their design. Before he and Anna moved to their present home, he was head gardener at nearby Chilcombe House. The cottage initially attracted them because it came with a workshop conveniently located in the buildings of the Edwardian model farm that also belongs to the estate. Having been unoccupied for some time, the cottage itself was unappealing, its walls sooty with mould, its floors covered in cheap, swirly carpet, but the setting was irresistible. 'It was summer when we first saw it and Anna and I lay in the long grass in the garden, listening to the buzzards mewing overhead. The house was very scruffy, but the place was a delight.'

Slotted into the side of a hill, the cottage is built on what Malcolm thinks is probably a medieval strip lynchet, the local name for a terrace cut into sloping land for farming. The garden extends sideways and

ABOVE LEFT In the larger of the two living rooms, the sofa sits against the matchboarded wall that boxes in the staircase. The pictures above the sofa are either by friends or junk shop finds, while the curving feathers are all that remain of Nimrod, the cockerel who attacked one of the children but provided a delicious dinner. Doors on the right lead into the kitchen, 'the boys' loo' and the larder where hangs a flitch of cured bacon from the pig they kept as part of a community pig project.

ABOVE Also in the living room hangs 'a rare Malcolm Seal', a painting of a pear dating back to his art school days. The shelves hold a teapot by potter Ursula Mommens, who is the great-granddaughter of Charles Darwin, fragments of Roman glass and a yellow slipware bowl that was a wedding present.

RIGHT The kitchen is too small for dining, so this is the room where they eat, at a table against the window, again affording that glorious view. Shelves above an old pine sideboard hold an ostrich egg given to Anna by a pupil and a stuffed squirrel that is one of Malcolm's more recent acquisitions.

is as productive as it is pretty, with fruit trees, a vegetable garden, a polytunnel festooned with tomatoes and chillis and handsome Black Rock chickens that regularly provide eggs. Closer to the house are topiary hawthorn trees, and a large yew teapot, of which Malcolm is particularly proud, having grown it from a seedling, the parent being a venerable Great Dixter yew. 'Cottage gardens often aped the design of country house gardens, and I felt this particular yew was destined to be a teapot,' says Malcolm fondly.

In front of the cottage the view stretches down and away over the valley towards a row of graceful poplars, their lower trunks wrapped in a thickly tapered padding of ivy, and to the gently rounded hills beyond them. In the distance you can see the flat-topped, stepped hill of an iron-age fort. 'The Romans built a road all the way from Dorchester in order to pacify that fort,' says Malcolm, 'and the floor of

my workshop is made from one of those poplars that blew down. It's the wood they always used for the floor of farm carts because it doesn't splinter when you scrape it.'

The garden has been brought back to life by hard work, but Malcolm says they have done very little to the interior of the cottage. Fortunately, Anna managed to persuade the landlord to paint the rooms before they moved in, thereby getting rid of the mould. But it was Anna and her mother who spent a day on hands and knees with scalpels and scrubbing brushes, cleaning the terracotta floor tiles that they found under the swirly carpet. Their only structural alteration was to the tiny fireplace in the smaller living room, which they call the snug. Here they have installed a proportionately small wood-burning stove. There is no central heating, only this stove, a Rayburn in the kitchen that also heats the water and a night storage heater on the landing.

The simple French provincial bench was spotted in a local junk shop and bought by the couple as their joint Christmas present. On the wall is a floating lady by Stephen Darragh, with whom Malcolm was at art college. The old Welsh blanket is woven in narrow strips sewn together, putting its date at pre-1900, after which wider looms were used. The cushion and lampshade are from Lush Designs.

'We didn't have much furniture when we first arrived,' says Malcolm, 'but we have slowly gathered things, mostly from markets and junk shops.' One of the few pieces they had was their double bed, which Malcolm made and Anna helped to design, using ash grown in Hooke Park. The bed almost fills the bedroom, but there is just room beside it for one of their more recent acquisitions, spotted in a junk shop. It is a bench, probably French, made of beech, with its original rush seat, each strand beautifully wrapped, as Malcolm points out, in a glossy, golden covering of split straw.

Here, as elsewhere, there are artworks by friends or artists whose work Malcolm admires; some acquired when Malcolm was still at art college, others bartered for baskets. Most have a strong flavour of the countryside, whether a study of stormy clouds or a close-up of hands picking hops. Downstairs is an etching of autumn plants by Robin Tanner, an engraving of the Chillingham bull by Thomas Bewick and a tiny woodcut of snowdrops by Ronald Stone, the artist who designed the logo for *The Times*, and the old five-pound note.

Each find has a story attached to it: a stunning drawing bought for £2, a fragment of a Chinese statuette and a face from a medieval bellarmine found in the mud of the Thames, a Persian helmet given to Malcolm by a man who found it in Baghdad, honed flints from antique guns and an ostrich egg given to Anna by a pupil. Even the cereal bowls come with a provenance, carved by a man in the village from the wood of one of a group of four sycamores known locally as Matthew, Mark, Luke and John, now with one missing.

Vegetables come from the garden; wood from the surrounding land. The kitchen shelves are old wooden crates and hanging in the larder is a flitch of home-cured ham from the pig they reared in a community project. Probably the most expensive things in the house are the lampshades by Lush Designs, although even these are seconds. 'The boys love them because they are covered in pictures of animals,' says Malcolm.

ABOVE Built as a barn in a farmyard now occupied by a stonemason, a blacksmith and a furniture restorer, Malcolm's two-storey workshop is as picturesque as his cottage and spacious enough to hold his popular weekend basket-making courses. Numbers are limited to six so that each trainee basket-maker gets individual attention.

BELOW Malcolm explains that cottage gardens often aped the gardens of grander houses, including features such as topiary on a smaller scale, and using plants like hawthorn as well as the more traditional yew. He is particularly proud of this teapot, which he grew from a seedling produced by one of the famous yews at Great Dixter.

CHARACTER
finishing touches

• PATINA This is key to the character of an interior. Skim an old plaster wall with new plaster and you have instantly lost all traces of the hands that first laid it and a precious link with the past. Both Jane Moran and Gerry Peachey have stripped later paper off old plaster walls and decided to leave the resulting layers of mottled paint untouched; like a coloured map revealing the history of generations of decoration.

• MORE PATINA If your interior has no intrinsic patina, either because it has already been obliterated or because the building is too new, you can find ways to import it. When Gerry Peachey built a new extension onto his early 19th-century cottage, he fitted its interior with salvaged doors, complete with antique handles and locks, and built a wall separating the back hall from the utility room using matchboarding from a redundant fire station, with its original blue paint.

• PATTERN Painting pattern directly onto plaster walls is an ancient form of decoration, used by Charlotte Molesworth – oak leaves in the kitchen: paisley in the living room – and by Gerry Peachey, who took the inspiration for the design on his bedroom wall from a photograph of a fragment of 17th-century leather wall hanging. Hand-painted patterns can be equally effective on floors; whether

the strict geometry of Jane Moran's black and white chequerboard or the wild zebra stripes of Gerry Peachey's landing.

• BUDGET Style need not be expensive. Every cottage in this chapter has been furnished and decorated on an extremely tight budget. Curtains are second-hand; furnishings homemade or at least home-modified. Some things have been bartered for, Gerry Peachey built some wardrobes in exchange for a flower painting, while Malcolm Seal made a basket in exchange for an antique linen sheet. Think what you might be prepared to swap for something you would love to own.

• SALVAGE Everyone in this chapter uses things they have found or salvaged, whether the wooden fruit boxes used as shelving in Malcolm Seal's kitchen or the old bricks dug up from the garden and now laid as flooring in Charlotte Molesworth's living room. Reusing and recycling things creatively is both green and stylish.

• IMPERFECTION Don't necessarily disregard something because it is broken or damaged. Perfection tends to be expensive, while a small chip or crack in a beautiful piece of china or pottery, for example, may make it affordable without detracting from its charm.

'*When I was down beside the sea*
A wooden spade they gave to me
To dig the sandy shore.
My holes were empty like a cup;
In every hole the sea came up,
Till it could come no more.'

ROBERT LOUIS STEVENSON (1850-1894)

HOLIDAY

HOLIDAYS AND THE SEASIDE ARE INDELIBLY
LINKED IN THE ENGLISH IMAGINATION. ALL THE
HOUSES IN THIS CHAPTER ARE CLOSE TO THE SEA
AND, ALTHOUGH TWO ARE WEEKEND RETREATS,
ONE IS A PERMANENT HOME WITH A HOLIDAY
FEEL. THIS ELUSIVE, CAREFREE ATMOSPHERE
IS AS MUCH A RESULT OF HOW YOU INHABIT A
HOUSE AS HOW YOU DECORATE IT: FURNISHINGS
ROBUST ENOUGH TO WITHSTAND ENTHUSIASTIC
DOGS AND CHILDREN; DOORS PROPPED OPEN
WHENEVER THE WEATHER ALLOWS; TABLES AND
CHAIRS FOR ALFRESCO MEALS; NOTHING TOO
PRISTINE OR PRECIOUS; AND A BUCKET AND
SPADE AT THE READY.

LEFT From the outside, the building looks like an ancient cottage with its weathered boarding and heavy thatch. Climbing plants, including the white rose *Félicité Perpétue,* add their scent and soft greenery to the rustic facade.

FAR LEFT The exterior hides an interior of surprising light and space. The building once housed dairy cows and Philip Wagner has opened it up to its original dimensions. The chairs are from IKEA and have been painted pale grey.

BELOW In the same room, a collection of napkin rings from a 1930s ocean liner is ranked on the brick chimney breast. The painted side table is French.

CAST-IRON EXCUSE

London-based architect and interior designer Philip Wagner set about searching for a country retreat in a methodical manner. He decided on an area near to the sea in Sussex, and even before seeing this house, it was close to the top of his list because of its proximity to an unspoilt stretch of coast.

When Philip poked his head through the hatch into the loft space of the house, he knew he had found what he was looking for. The exterior of the house presents an architectural puzzle. It comprises one end of a long, single-storey, L-shaped building clad in weathered timber, with small, low windows and a heavy hood of thatch. Its age is indeterminate, its use a mystery: rustic almshouses, perhaps, or a rare example of a tasteful, vernacular bungalow. In fact, the building dates from the 1930s and was built using reclaimed materials in a deliberately old-fashioned style as the dairy of a farm built at the same time and part of a large and wealthy estate. What Philip saw when he peered into the loft was the unusual internal structure of the building, the cast-iron

beams and the tops of cast-iron pillars supporting them. Being an architect, what he immediately recognized was the potential for opening up the space and making this cast-iron framework a feature of the interior.

'I immediately loved the location,' Philip expands. 'It feels so remote, but in fact is only a short drive from the nearest supermarket, and there is a wonderful, wild shingle beach just two fields away. But inside the house it was dark and rather suburban with fitted carpet everywhere, low ceilings and woodwork stained brown. The pillars had been bricked in to make them square, but I could see the tops of them rising from the attic floor and all that space and volume just going to waste.'

Philip bought the house and began the process of de-suburbanizing, stripping out

the ceilings, installing stone and timber floors and making new openings in the walls so that the rooms flow into one another. On either side of the entrance hall are the kitchen and dining room. 'Both these rooms were originally bullpens,' Philip explains, 'and had incredibly thick, concrete walls, so cutting through from the dining room into the sitting room and the kitchen into the utility room was a major operation.'

The central living room is the most dramatic of the recently liberated spaces, its already generous floor area given double the impact by the extra ceiling height. Another quirk of the building's construction is that the thatch rises steeply to a flat, felted roof in the middle and this allowed Philip to cut out two large skylights, effectively banishing the former

ABOVE As well as opening up the interior by removing the ceilings that were installed when the building was first converted, Philip Wagner has created wide openings between the reception rooms so that the space and light flow between them. The dining room, to the right of the picture, and the kitchen, which opens off the other side of the entrance hall, were both built as bullpens and had thick concrete walls. The flooring is reconstituted stone and has heating laid beneath it.

RIGHT The sitting room has French doors that open into the garden. The armchair is Victorian, covered in natural linen, and the table lamp was bought in France. Also on the table is some of Philip's collection of cocktail shakers. 'One on its own wouldn't look very interesting,' he says, 'but I love the look of them clustered in a group.'

gloom. He filled the end wall with floor-to-ceiling shelving, made by a local carpenter and painted white, and he clad the inside of the roof with sawn pine boarding, each board carefully aged and distressed before being fixed in place in order to ensure a convincingly uneven finish. 'It's not easy to get this kind of distressing just right,' says Philip, 'but I always use Sarah Patey, and she is brilliant at it.'

Sarah Patey's skill is evident elsewhere in the house. Thanks to her ability to endow the brand new with an instant patina of mellow age, Philip was able to keep and transform the 'horrible' kitchen units, and put with them a kitchen table and chairs from IKEA. Sarah also painted a pair of white Lloyd Loom-style armchairs with a subtle wash of grey and dulled down the bright aluminium of the pendant lights in the kitchen, also from IKEA, to a matt grey that looks more like old zinc.

Distressed, worn paintwork is a leitmotif, some of it the genuine result of long wear and tear, some courtesy of Sarah Patey. 'I knew exactly the look I wanted to create here,' says Philip, 'a mix of New

LEFT Most of the furnishings that are not antique are from IKEA, in some cases, like the kitchen table and chairs, painted and distressed by Sarah Patey. The metal ceiling lamps, also from IKEA, have been patinated by Sarah to look like old zinc. Lined up on the windowsill are vintage soda syphons, which, in common with the cocktail shakers, Philip likes to display en masse. The utility room is screened from the kitchen by a simple curtain.

TOP RIGHT Open shelving in the kitchen holds tidy ranks of glasses. Also stored here is the everyday crockery; a mixed batch, including some antique items, unified by a strict colour code of blue and white.

RIGHT Oars and paddles, bought in local boot fairs and propped in the entrance hall, are for display rather than use and contribute to the sporting, outdoors feel of the cottage. The painted Swedish clock was another boot fair find. The imitation stone flooring was installed by Philip to replace the previous wall-to-wall fitted carpeting.

England and Southern France, with a bit of Swedish thrown in.' The Swedish is partly in honour of Philip's wife, Liskulla, who is a Swedish psychologist. Perhaps fortunately for Philip, she has no interest in spending time on interior design, leaving him free to indulge his vision on his own. And, as interior design forms an important part of his work, as well as being his personal passion, he undertook it with the benefit of long experience and a well-practised eye.

He reckons it took about three months to furnish the house, plus another nine months or so gathering finishing touches. Armed with a scale plan showing the positions and rough dimensions of the furniture he wanted, and including the placing of lamps, he embarked on a buying spree that he describes as 'verging on frenzied'. Antique fairs in France and Britain, flea markets in Paris and local boot fairs were all scoured for interesting pieces, while IKEA filled in the gaps. 'I think of myself as quite a versatile designer, a bit of a chameleon,' Philip comments. 'I like modern, art deco, and more traditional styles, and am always interested to work with a client's taste and preferences. But the one thing I am not is minimalist. I like stuff.'

The house is stuffed with stuff, albeit so stylishly arranged that the effect is more poised than cluttered. Various collections fill surfaces and shelves: sporting trophies, shiny cocktail shakers glinting on a side table, soda siphons lined up on a windowsill. Ranked on the stepped brick of the chimney breast, there are dozens of ivorine napkin rings, each with a number, from a 1930s passenger liner. Contributing to the breezy, sporty, seaside feel are model boats, crossed oars mounted on a wall, lobster pots by the front door, and in the hall a clustering of golf clubs, tennis rackets and fishing gear. Philip Wagner says he is not at all sporty, nor does he enjoy drinking cocktails; it's all to create an ambience rather than to be used. 'I wanted the place to have a really relaxed, holiday atmosphere. It's a house for lolling around and reading the Sunday papers after a walk on the beach.'

ABOVE Philip Wagner lined this bathroom with rough sawn pine boarding, painted with a thin coat of emulsion. The washbasin with its integral surround was another IKEA purchase in a now-discontinued design. Built-in shelves hold books, china and a group of antique chemist's bottles, as well as the tooth mug.

LEFT This spare bedroom has walls enlivened with a drapery of vintage bunting. The bedspreads are from IKEA. The planked doors with strap hinges are echoed in the style of the corner wardrobe.

In another spare bedroom, the double bed fits neatly beneath an alcove created by the differing ceiling heights and flanked on one side by one of the cast-iron columns that support the roof. The bedspread and cushions are from IKEA.

LEFT The main bedroom houses a long wardrobe designed by Philip with the same planked doors and elegant strap hinges that are a leitmotif throughout the cottage. The contrast between the rustic woodwork and the industrial feel of the cast-iron supporting columns and network of riveted girders, gives the interior an architectural interest that had been disguised by previous owners under false ceilings and brick cladding. The oversized white pots arranged along the top of the wardrobes include a milk churn and a chimney pot.

ABOVE The same bedroom has a door opening straight into the garden, one of the benefits of one-storey living.

CORNISH DREAM

If, as you sit in your urban office in front of a blinking computer screen, you ever find yourself daydreaming about life in the perfect cottage, in perfect countryside, you might come up with something that looks very much like this. Rose and Johnny Bamford's Cornish home is ridiculously picturesque. Leaving main roads behind, the drive there takes you across exposed pasture where trees are sharply angled by the wind, and on towards the sea into deep, narrow lanes. Just before you reach the house, the single track squeezes into the dip of a tiny wooded valley, its steep sides fringed by bracken, a fast, rocky brook bubbling along next to the cracked tarmac.

LEFT Johnny Bamford and a friend rebuilt this part of the cottage, which probably dates back to the 16th century and was a ruin consisting of little more than a chimney stack and a stone doorway. Inside is now a double-height kitchen and living room.

The entrance hall and staircase is in the later farmhouse that sits at right angles to the earlier building and has been linked to it by a curving corridor. This part of the house had been inhabited, but was semi-derelict when Johnny bought it. The grain bin holds some of Rose's fabric collection, the Mexican metal wall cabinet miniature finds including Victorian celluloid Christmas decorations.

ABOVE When Rose moved in with Johnny, the house was a bachelor pad and this room was used solely for parties. Gradually she has lightened and feminized the space, adding her own touches, such as these pretty teacups that hang above a window.

RIGHT The old stone arched doorway opens into the light and space of the kitchen and living room, which has two storeys of windows and big ceiling skylights. One end of the room has a slightly raised floor level. Here, the simple kitchen units were designed by Rose and Johnny and made by local joiners. The intricate cut-out picture by Rob Ryan to the right of the door was a birthday present from Johnny to Rose.

BELOW Dandy Star's popular 'Love' poster hangs over the sink next to the pistachio green Aga, which was a wedding present. The ceiling lights are from Habitat; the wall lights were made by Rose using old buttons threaded onto wire. Rose also painstakingly grouted the mosaic tiling in grey to complement its dusky mauve.

As you crawl up out of the trees onto high ground, the sea appears, a misty line in the distance, and the Bamfords' driveway hooks down to the right. The house looks as though it has grown out of the landscape. The low facade is local slate, the Tudor doorway set into a granite surround. The slate roof is mottled with moss and lichen, its eaves blurred by the plants that grow up the walls and frame the windows. The surrounding garden of thick, tufty grass and squat stone walls is peppered with toys, small Wellington boots and abandoned bicycles. And facing the house is Rose's studio where she screen-prints prototypes for the t-shirts and posters she and her friend Charlotte Day sell under the name Dandy Star to trendy boutiques. Their 'Love' poster, in particular, has the style cachet of that once attached to Venetian glass mirrors — a *sine qua non* of the fashionable Notting Hill interior.

Behind the old-fashioned charm of slate and granite and small-paned cottage windows, the house hides a surprise that is the architectural equivalent of a pre-war Bentley with an eight-litre engine. The heavy oak door opens not into the dark, flagged hall you might expect but instead into a single, bright space that reaches up to the roof beams and is drenched with light from three large skylights even on the greyest winter day. This room is the heart of the house; kitchen, dining and living room, with an Aga at one end and a huge granite fireplace at the other, somehow combining all the character and cosiness of an ancient cottage, with the space and glamour of an urban loft.

Ten years ago, when Rose Bamford sold her London flat and committed herself to Johnny and country life, the house looked much the same from the outside, but was a very different creature within. What is not immediately apparent is that there are two houses, which sit very close and at right angles. Until Johnny bought them, one was a ruin, the other semi-derelict. The story of their purchase goes back to his childhood when he used to come to listen to the tales of the old farmer who lived in one room and kept animals in the other.

FAR LEFT One step down from the kitchen area is a Victorian dining table, recently painted pale grey by Rose. Beneath its tasteful loose cover made from antique French linen sheets, the giant sofa is red and a survivor from the days when this room was the venue for Johnny's legendary parties. The original fireplace, framed by slabs of local granite with sofa and armchairs gathered in front of it, makes this room the ultimate modern farmhouse kitchen; a multi-purpose space where children and adults can cook, play, eat and relax. The high-level alcove in the chimney breast was once a smaller bedroom fireplace.

LEFT An inherited Victorian rocking chair pulled up to the fire invites you to settle down on a winter afternoon with a good book and feet on the fender.

BELOW The three family bedrooms are in the later of the two buildings, which retains its second storey. The bed in Pearl's room, home to numerous teddy bears, is a family heirloom.

Stories of Johnny's youth, his circus-trained Palomino horse that he used to ride into the pub and make kneel at the bar, his Cuban heels, his partying, make it clear he was never a typical farmer's boy. Twenty-five years ago, having bought both the old farmhouse and the ruin next door, Johnny and a friend set about restoring them. They reconstructed the ruin around its ancient chimney stack and stone doorway, the only parts of this miniature Elizabethan manor that were still standing, and added a curved, single-storey corridor linking the houses to make a single, L-shaped building.

'Johnny lived in the house he restored, but the bit that had been a ruin became his party house – a big space with an open fire and a mezzanine bedroom floor where people crashed out,' says Rose. 'He was a confirmed bachelor and knew a few key

London people, and he used to entertain what seemed like the whole of West London. When I first arrived, every nook and cranny in this bit of the house had a bottle top or a fag end stuffed into it, and the carpet smelled like an old beer mat. All the beams and doors were stained mahogany brown and the place was stuffed with old pews, plaster statues of nuns and other bits of Victorian gothic that he had inherited from a friend who lived in a Methodist chapel.'

Rose set about transforming the house and domesticating Johnny. 'Every time he went to London I got out a pot of white paint,' she laughs. Ten years on and the party house is as stylish as it is family friendly. The mezzanine has been removed, the concrete floor replaced by oak boards and the exposed stone of the chimney breast plastered over and painted white. A giant sofa faces the fire and is a rare survivor from the party days, now sobered up with a loose cover made from antique linen sheets.

At the far end of this lofty space, a door leads to a bathroom and a bedroom. At the other end, the new curved corridor leads to the house next door, which has a more conventional layout with three bedrooms upstairs. Even in their absence, it isn't difficult to guess which room belongs to their daughter Pearl, who has a taste for pink and fairies, and their son Frankie, whose bed is a more masculine gloss black.

The transformation of the house was gradual, but is now complete. In the place of gothic kitsch there are paintings by Rose's father, artist Timothy Gibbs, and artworks by other friends, including delicate cutwork by Rob Ryan and objets trouvés decorated by Rose's friend and business partner Charlotte Day. 'Pretty much everything in the house has been handed down from family, or given to us,' says Rose. 'I only ever buy things if they are very cheap.'

In the summer Rose says they are inundated by visitors. 'It's always lovely to see friends,' she says, 'but it does sometimes feel like running a free B&B. They probably think "Oh, lucky her, in this big, flash house in such a beautiful place"'. They almost certainly do.

ABOVE This downstairs bedroom is part of Johnny's new extension and used to be the workshop from where he ran a business selling wetsuits and surfboards. Although completely untrained, Johnny seems to have a natural feel for building and architecture, and the alterations and additions he made to the two neglected houses he bought all those years ago are indistinguishable from the original structures. Now converted for guests, this room houses the elegant brass bed that belonged to Rose's parents and that Rose thinks she was probably born in.

LEFT In the same bedroom, the doll's house also dates back to Rose's childhood. Pictures propped on the shelf are by Rose and by her father, the artist Timothy Gibbs.

This downstairs bathroom is next to the guest bedroom. Rose says that space for guests is essential, as in summer they are inundated by friends from London, desperate to exchange dusty pavements for the space and fresh sea air of the Cornish coast. Propped in a corner is a piece of driftwood found and painted by Rose's friend and business partner Charlotte Day when they were on holiday together in Mallorca.

SEASIDE BOARDING

There is something almost poetic in the way Elizabeth Machin talks about North Norfolk. 'As a family we holidayed there. My artist mother loved the three-quarter skies, and my birdwatcher brothers paced the shingle at dawn. It was the seascape that grabbed me, and how you could walk the flat shores.'

TOP LEFT The kitchen opens straight into the back garden, perfect for breakfast on a summer morning. The combination of flint and brick, topped by undulating pantiles, is typical of Norfolk cottage architecture.

LEFT The dark polished metal of the cast-iron Victorian fireplace makes a strong visual focus in the living room. Hanging on the matchboarding that Elizabeth installed and that clads one wall of the room is a driftwood sculpture by Karen Miller. The concertinaed linocut of birds and trees on the mantelpiece is by printmaker Linda Farquharson.

TOP RIGHT A small, planked cupboard in the corner of the room, is painted in the same Farrow & Ball 'Elephant's Breath' as the matchboarding. The group of little celadon pots are from a local pottery, Made in Cley, and the ceramic tray is from Abigail Ahern. 'If things are slightly pared down,' says Elizabeth, 'then you seem to appreciate objects like a simple jug of hedgerow flowers or a few handcrafted ceramics.'

A couple of years ago, Elizabeth Machin's dream of finding a Norfolk 'bolt-hole' was realized when she and her husband bought a Victorian brick and flint cottage in a village a short drive from the coast. 'We had been on a lot of lists for quite a long time when this came up. It was in the right place and was the right price, and we bought it shockingly fast just before Christmas. It was like getting a fantastic early present.'

Past the church and the pond, the cottage is one of a terrace of five, each with two white windows, one downstairs, one up, and unified by a deep roof of ridged terracotta tiles. The exterior is plain, set a few feet back from the pavement behind plain railings, and not much more than 3.6 m (12 ft) wide. The planked front door opens straight into

The front door opens into the living room, which stretches the width of the cottage. The sofa bed, from K A International, was the largest that would fit through the door. The elegant wooden love seat was 'an indulgence' from Margaret Howell and the coffee table is from Walker Restoration. On the left of the front door is a photograph of a Norfolk seascape.

BEACH

LEFT The cottage is in a small village a few miles inland from the Norfolk coast, which Elizabeth remembers from childhood holidays and that drew her back to this part of the country, so the sign pointing to the beach by the back door from the kitchen is not entirely inaccurate. The matchboarding that clads the fireplace wall of the living room is continued around three walls of the kitchen, but ends at eye level in this room, providing a shelf for display and storage.

BELOW The narrow wooden staircase is boxed in and leads up from the living room. The stripey stair runner is from Roger Oates. The antique bench on the landing was bought from an antiques shop on Camden Passage.

the living room, from where a door leads through into the kitchen. Upstairs are two bedrooms and a bathroom, and there is a third attic bedroom in the roof. 'It's really very small,' says Elizabeth, 'but that suits us. The boys share, and we still have a spare room for guests to stay in.'

Having bought the house so quickly, Elizabeth decided to 'let it sleep for a while'. This gave her time to plan how to furnish and decorate it, and to wait for a local craftsman builder whose work had been highly recommended by a friend. 'We didn't need to do anything structural, but the interior was dark and dingy and we decided to rip out the kitchen and bathroom, take up the carpets and redecorate throughout.' Such was their trust in the builder, Chas Major, that they felt able to hand him the cottage keys and drive home to London. 'Every so often we would have nice chats about how it was going. He immediately understood the look we wanted and often made his own suggestions.'

Starting the decoration and furnishing of a house from scratch, is a design luxury. Elizabeth has particularly well-developed ideas about interior design and, as a PR consultant, up-to-date knowledge of what is available. Her clients include Bennison Fabrics, Anta and Alternative Flooring, all of whose products she has used in the cottage.

The kitchen has a slate floor and simple wooden panelled cupboards made by their 'fantastic builder and craftsman' Chas Major to a design by Elizabeth. Propped on a shelf are three unfinished seacapes by friend and artist Jonathan Millward, painted on a visit to the cottage and left behind as a present. An antique coarse linen runner from Beyond France lies across the table.

On the first floor are two bedrooms and a bathroom, with a spare bedroom in the attic. Elizabeth has used the same matchboarding as downstairs to line one wall of each bedroom, and together with the muted palette of blues, greys, greens and browns, this helps unify the interior of the cottage and increase the sense of space.

In order to give the rooms a linking architectural motif, she decided to clad some of the upstairs and downstairs walls with painted matchboarding. 'We didn't want to go for the too rustic or the twee seaside look,' she says 'but the boards give the rooms a simple, country feel and make them cosy in the same way that wooden panelling does. It's traditional, but not overtly old-fashioned.'

In London, the family live in a terraced Victorian house that Elizabeth has decorated in pale, gentle colours, which she describes as 'slightly Swedish'. This is also the palette she has chosen for Norfolk. 'When I am planning a colour scheme,' she says, 'I imagine a favourite view, which is always shaped by the sea and sky. In the cottage we have used watery sky blues, soft greys, celadon green and driftwood browns. These are shades that flow naturally together and help to increase the sense of space.'

Furnishings have been equally carefully selected. 'I wanted to keep it simple, and to use eco-friendly materials and local craftsmen wherever possible,' says Elizabeth. The living room floor is light golden oak, softened by a layering of two natural rugs. Comfortable seating and an extra bed are provided by the largest sofa bed that would fit through the front door. 'Lack of space means you have to be very selective, and because we chose a large sofa for the sake of comfort, other pieces had to be relatively small,' comments Elizabeth. The neat armchair earned its place because of its size, and the wooden love seat, 'an indulgence' from Margaret Howell, because of its delicate silhouette.

Cushions, throws, lamps and decorative objects all accord with this same calm, pared-down aesthetic. A ring of driftwood, like a pale sunburst, hangs over the fireplace, and there is an elegant grouping of celadon pots and a plain cream vase on a cabinet, some of which are presents from Elizabeth's mother bought from the pottery in nearby Cley. 'We come for weekends and for holidays as often as we can,' says Elizabeth. 'But my mother also comes and my brothers and friends, and people often leave things for the house, like the unfinished seascapes in the kitchen that are painted by an artist friend, Jonathan Millward.'

As befits a holiday house so close to the sea, there are bowls of pebbles and shells, weathered bones, fanned-out seaweed, seedpods and pine cones. 'I want us all to find a few things and let the place evolve over time.'

FAR LEFT The unusual blue chest with its square drawers was another find from Walker Restoration. Downstairs the flooring is oak boards in the living room and slate in the kitchen, but for upstairs Elizabeth chose fitted carpet in a neutral shade from Alternative Flooring, with rugs also from Alternative Flooring laid on top. Looking across the landing there is a view into the bathroom.

LEFT All the beds, including those in the boys' bedroom, are from All in Wood. The checked bed linen is from Aspace. A photo of Alexander, the older of the two boys, hangs over his bed.

Theo's bed fits neatly into the corner of the same bedroom, again marked by a photograph of him hanging on the wall above. The window, as in all the rooms, has shutters instead of curtains, in accordance with Elizabeth's vision for the interior as 'simple and natural, calm and cosy'.

HOLIDAY
finishing touches

• FLOORING For a house to have a leisurely atmosphere, it needs to be a place where you can feel relaxed and not permanently on edge about a smattering of dirt or mild chaos. Practical flooring is important and on the ground floor should be designed to withstand summer sand and winter mud. Wooden floors are particularly forgiving, especially old boards that have already taken a battering. Original or reclaimed flagstones are even better – dirt just seems to disappear.

• STRIPEY WALLS Ice cream pastels like pistachio green, primrose yellow or pale strawberry pink have a summery beach-hut look, especially when used on walls and painted in wide stripes on a white background. This is a relatively easy DIY task, using masking tape to encourage straight lines and sharp edges.

• STRIPEY FABRICS Similarly, fabrics in bold deckchair stripes have an informal, breezy feel. Blue and white stripes are unfailingly fresh and nautical.

• OBJETS TROUVES Who can spend an afternoon on a beach without picking up shells and pebbles or pieces of driftwood? These should be rigorously edited before being hauled home, but the best ones might find their place on a windowsill or collected in a bowl. Little shells look pretty in glass bottles, while big pebbles make excellent paperweights, even doorstops.

• MATCHBOARDING Painted matchboarding is the humblest form of interior panelling and appropriate for a cottage, whether used to clad a wall up to dado level, or from floor to ceiling, as in Elizabeth Machin's cottage. As well as adding architectural character to an interior, a wooden lining gives a room a cosy, shipshape feel, like a captain's cabin.

• SPORT Philip Wagner has filled his seaside cottage with old-fashioned sporting paraphernalia; from wooden tennis racquets and vintage golf clubs to fishing nets and oars, all picked up for a song at local markets. While he cheerfully admits that none of them are used, their presence brings the outdoors inside as effectively as flinging open all the doors and windows.

• INFORMALITY With her artist's eye, Rose Bamford has a talent for mixing junk shop finds, children's art and the homemade with the antique, for an effect as apparently casual as it is visually pleasing. When grouping disparate objects, colour and proportion are key and endless experiment is necessary to get the desired result.

• HOME Two of the three cottages in this chapter are holiday and weekend retreats; one a permanent home. To make a second home feel loved and lived-in, make sure it contains some favourite things; build and edit its contents over months and years, rather than in the space of a week's frantic buying and bring with you fresh flowers or a pot of geraniums whenever you visit.

'*Then past his dark white cottage front*
A labourer went along, his tread
Slow, half with weariness, half with ease;
And, through the silence, from his shed
The sound of sawing rounded all
That silence said.'

EDWARD THOMAS (1878-1917)

SIMPLICITY

WELL OVER A CENTURY AGO, WILLIAM MORRIS
WAS CAMPAIGNING FOR CRAFTSMANSHIP AND
QUALITY IN THE FACE OF MASS PRODUCTION.
HIS MOST FAMOUS HOUSEHOLD EDICT ABOUT
ONLY FURNISHING A HOUSE WITH 'WHAT YOU
KNOW TO BE USEFUL, OR BELIEVE TO BE
BEAUTIFUL' COULD SAFELY BE APPLIED TO
THE COTTAGES IN THIS CHAPTER. WITH THEIR
CAREFULLY EDITED CONTENTS, CELEBRATION OF
THE HANDMADE, AND THEIR EMPHASIS ON THE
UNADORNED APPEAL OF NATURAL MATERIALS,
THEY CAPTURE THE SPIRIT OF PRE-INDUSTRIAL
'HONEST LABOUR' WITHOUT SACRIFICING A JOT
OF MODERN COMFORT.

PLAIN DEALING

This four-storey, Georgian terraced house on a wide, elegant street not far from Waterloo Station shouldn't strictly be included in a book about cottages. It is too urban and a bit too grand. But it has qualities that give it honorary cottage status. As owners John Hall and Robert Hirschhorn are keen to point out, this area of London, which now seems so central, was a country village when the house was built and its narrow garden was backed by fields, the parish church a short, leafy walk away.

ABOVE A gravel path leads down the long, lush garden to a modern studio where the overflow stock of antique country furniture is on display. The door to the dining room stands ajar and steps lead to the sitting room.

BELOW The kitchen opens off the dining room and is painted in Farrow & Ball 'Light Grey' against a background of Farrow & Ball 'Pea Green' on the walls. The painted cupboard is early 19th-century bohemian.

RIGHT Above the dining room fireplace hangs an 18th-century glazed overdoor with the monogram 'TLC' in curling letters of lead. The folk art watercolour portraits of a husband and wife date from about 1830 and the chair is late 18th century.

ABOVE The table is an 18th-century oak and ash Welsh farmhouse table, its top bearing the scars of many years of use. Fitted shelves hold a collection of 19th-century spongeware. The room is painted in Farrow & Ball 'Off White', with 'Light Grey' woodwork.

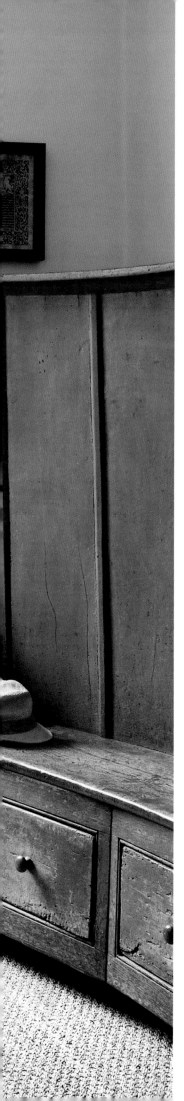

LEFT The drawing room has a sash window that also functions as a door into the garden and a mix of furnishings that juxtaposes the rustic with the refined. In the former category is the late 18th-century, blue-painted settle with its comfortably curved back and chunky drawers, in the latter the Adam-influenced gilt mirror of a similar date. The picture above the settle is an incredibly intricate cut-paper Lord's Prayer, dated 1801.

RIGHT The parlour at the front of the house has a similarly diverse mix of contents. The original ochre paint of the North Country lambing chair is picked up in the gold of the early 20th-century yellow silk damask curtains. The fruitwood and oak long-case clock dates from around 1750 and the room, including the floor, is painted in four different 'Stone' colours, all from Papers and Paints.

In 1809 it was described as 'a pleasant retreat for those citizens who have a taste for the country'. And, while the house is tall and the ceilings of the ground and first floor rooms are lofty, they are sandwiched between a kitchen and dining room in the half-basement, and bedrooms and a bathroom on the top floor, all with distinctly cottagey proportions.

The structure of the house bears witness to its rustic past. The street was developed at the end of the 18th century, when the manor house at the bottom of the road was demolished and its bricks, stone and even timbers were recycled for use in the new houses. Country superstitions prompted the original builders to place a mummified rat in a cavity of the wall next to the dining room chimney breast, disinterred over 200 years later by John and Robert's builders. A mouse wrapped in string was found under the floorboards of a nearby property. All the ironwork, including the front railings, was hand-forged by the village blacksmith. 'It definitely has a country feeling,' John asserts.

But the real justification for slipping this graceful town house into a book about cottages is the way it has been furnished and the unlikely atmosphere of Hardyesque simplicity this conjures in what is now a profoundly urban setting only a stretch of pavement and a pinch point away from a Greek Taverna, a Turkish delicatessen, a bookmakers and a road thick with cars, lorries and double-decker buses. Sitting in the quiet back garden enfolded by greenery, you wouldn't be at all surprised to hear the bleating of sheep or the screech of a cockerel.

John Hall and Robert Hirschhorn are antique dealers. They specialize in early country furniture

BELOW Floors throughout the house are either seagrass matting or wooden boards, which in the main bedroom, seen here from the landing, are painted in a shade of 'Stone' from Papers and Paints. The carved oak chest is 17th-century English and the crewel work panel hanging behind it is early 18th century and notable for the beauty of its colours, which have barely faded.

ABOVE RIGHT At the top of the house the ceilings are much lower, as they are on the lower ground floor. The unusual table is a 19th-century cedar 'twig' table and the group of pictures are 19th- and early 20th-century family portraits and travel photographs.

FAR RIGHT The white crocheted bedcover in the main bedroom was made by one of John's New Zealand aunts, and the white table lamp is by Andrew Crouch. The late 19th-century crewel work panel hanging behind the bed is no less attractive for being unfinished.

and their house is their showroom. The kitchen table is Welsh, its top scored and scarred by generations of farmers' wives and their carving knives. The panelled parlour is home to a wooden shepherd's chair from Lancashire, now painstakingly stripped back to its original coat of mustard yellow paint, its solid rockers worn smooth on flagstones, its little drawer still ready to receive an orphaned lamb. A farmhouse settle takes the place of a sofa in the living room, while the mantelpiece displays a primitive floor brush, its organic bristles topped by moulded leather, hardened and darkened by age to the texture of old oak. Spongeware pottery and early Delft clusters on plain, fitted shelving, and the walls are dotted with rustic pictures of the homemade variety – samplers laboured over by little girls, charming collages assembled by amateur artists showing scenes of country life.

'In some ways,' says John Hall, 'I think our look is quite modern. Early country furniture tends to have simple lines and a minimum of fussy decoration. It's also very versatile and can look good in many contexts, from sun-filled California homes to Nantucket beach houses and London flats.' He might have added Georgian town houses to his list, as it is certainly shown to advantage in these plainly decorated, nicely proportioned rooms.

The extensive restoration of the house, which began eight years ago when John and Robert exchanged it for a smaller house a few doors away,

has only recently been finished, but is imperceptible to the extent that it has stripped the house back to its original structure. Aside from a rather luxurious bathroom, it would be easy to imagine that the house had remained untouched, bar decoration, since it was first built in 1776. Walls are painted in flat, neutral shades. The floorboards are painted or covered with seagrass. Window dressings are minimal cream roller blinds or shutters, except in the small front parlour where old silk curtains confer a faded grandeur.

In this slightly austere setting, the furniture and objects that are John and Robert's stock seem so at home that it is difficult to believe any one of them might have to be sent away to new owners as soon as tomorrow. Although most buyers make an appointment to visit, John and Robert also sell from their website. Only the other day an oak linen press was shipped off to Japan. Quite aside from the temporary inconvenience of losing your kitchen chairs or the chest of drawers you keep your underwear in, it must require a continual effort of aesthetic juggling to keep each room looking more like a home than a shop.

Part of the solution is a purpose-built studio at the bottom of the garden where the overflow can be stored and displayed, particularly pieces that are not English or that do not have an obvious place in the main house. But John admits that moving furniture and rearranging rooms has become second nature. It is also a relief

HERE AND RIGHT The top-floor
guest room encompasses a more
global mix of antiques, including a long
border of early 18th-century French
embroidered tambour work, its colours
still so fresh that it can never have been
used, an American gothic clock and a
Scandinavian mahogany chest by the
bed, both early 19th century. A pair of
needlework chairs and 'Wedding Cake'
lampshade represent Britain.

to learn that there are a few things they would
not sell: the 18th-century sweet jars on the chest of
drawers in the bedroom that were left to Robert by
a friend; the crocheted bedspread made by one of
John's aunts; the American miniature teddy bear on
the bedroom mantelpiece that belonged to Robert's
mother; and the Welsh oak corner cupboard in the
dining room that would leave nasty holes in the wall.

It must help that both are unfeasibly tidy, and
unsentimental. Robert's approach is that of a
scholar. His credentials include an MA from Yale
in medieval sculpture and an unfinished PhD at the
Courtauld on late medieval porch architecture. John
Hall, who left New Zealand 30 years ago 'having
read nothing but H.E. Bates, and dreaming of parish
churches and village greens', worked as a counsellor
before turning to antique dealing full time. He
seems more interested in the human stories behind
the pieces they buy, and has a sharp eye for folk art.
His current favourites are three early 19th-century
collage pictures by George Smart, also known as
'the Tailor of Frant', who used scraps of fabric
and leather to make jaunty portraits of local
characters. Their childlike charm gives them an
intimacy that brings the past to life in a way no
perfectly executed oil painting could.

The top floor of the house has the most personal and private feel, as it is least likely to be visited by clients. Family photographs are grouped on the wall and the small office is piled with papers, periodicals and books in a welcome flurry of mild disorder. Behind the office is a spare bedroom and next to it a bathroom. Over the door into the bedroom hangs a trio of little round pictures, framed in wood, that look from a distance like tasteful Regency miniatures. A closer inspection reveals that they are kitsch prints of children, which Robert has kept because they belonged to his father. Similarly incongruous are the Ware figurines of cute little boys with cheekily punning titles that belonged to John as a child. Needless to say, like the bedspread and the sweet jars, these are not for sale.

ABOVE RIGHT Looking along the landing towards the bathroom, the office is on the left and the guest bedroom is through the door next to the bathroom. The Regency scumble-glazed shelves hold family photographs and ornaments, including a Regency penwork box and an Irish Delft plate.

RIGHT The cockerel on the windowsill is an early 19th-century weathervane and the baskets are 19th-century Swedish. Walls are painted in Farrow & Ball 'White Tie', with wood-work in 'Buff', and the washbasin is 'London' from C.P. Hart.

LEFT The cottage is 17th century, possibly earlier, and has its back to the lane that winds its way through the village. The fact that a communal pump still stands on this side of the house suggests that there may once have been a public path through what is now the garden. The local stone in this part of Dorset is toffee coloured.

LIGHT FANTASTIC

In 1989 Cressida Granger and her future business partner David Mulley visited Edward Craven Walker, inventor and manufacturer of that cult 1960s product the lava lamp, at his nudist camp in Dorset. Cressida and David were dealers specializing in 1960s furniture and lighting, and their idea was to open a shop and sell new instead of second-hand lava lamps. An agreement was drawn up on a sheet of A4 paper, and five years later David and Cressida bought the company and renamed it Mathmos.

LEFT A pair of vintage leather chairs, their backs leaning at a rakish angle, join the big group of seating in the living room. Behind this one of the pair is a shop fitting from an old draper's shop, now used as storage for books. Another of these reclaimed fittings has found a new use in the kitchen. To the left of this view is the front door and also the staircase that would originally have been separated from the rest of the room by a partition wall.

Since 1999 Cressida Granger has owned and run Mathmos herself, and the range of lighting has continued to grow, while remaining innovative and high tech. It is a surprise to learn that this trend-spotting entrepreneur lives for much of the year in a thatched cottage in a far-flung corner of Dorset. She and her partner Chiara Nosarti, a neuro-psychologist, come here for weekends and for weeks on end in the summer. Admittedly, the Mathmos factories are based in Poole, but a traditional, almost chocolate-box cottage seems an unlikely home for someone whose work is cutting-edge, contemporary design.

BELOW The fireplace in the living room was reconstructed and the elm floorboards are new. The caned coffee table came from Cressida's grandfather, who was a doctor and used it as a bed for patients. The leather armchair in the foreground is by Matthew Hilton, the sofa is from SCP and the corduroy-covered tub chairs date from the 1930s.

RIGHT On the other side of the
staircase from the living room is
the room that Cressida and Chiara
use as an informal dining room
(the opening into the kitchen is just
visible on the left). The fireplace is
original and hanging from one of the
beams are outsized kitchen utensils,
including a huge colander given to
Cressida by her brother for collecting
apples. The stacked wooden chairs
are 1950s school chairs, which are
often needed for guests.

BELOW In the alcove on the right
of the dining room fireplace hangs
a strange Edwardian painting, a
detailed study of a small piece of tree
branch, given to Cressida and Chiara
by Cressida's parents and known
jokingly as 'the family twig'. The large
Victorian glass dome holds a temporary
arrangement of grasses, and there
are two small, tactile Mathmos lights
on the platter.

Cressida's eye for modernity does not mean that she is immune to
the charms of the countryside or the allure of period architecture.
The landscape surrounding her cottage in this pretty village of toffee-
coloured stone, thatch and mullioned windows is particularly appealing,
criss-crossed by lanes that have sunk so deep over the centuries that
their lush, green banks rise up on either side like the walls of tiny
railway cuttings. Then there are what Cressida calls the 'comedy hills';
perfect bell-shaped mounds, green as lime jelly, often topped with a
faintly ridiculous tuft of trees, and decorated by a sprinkling of cows
or sheep. 'I was brought up in Dorset,' Cressida explains, 'and my
family still lives in Dorset, and I feel at home here.'

They bought the house 11 years ago, but only after a long and
disheartening search. 'We would come down from London for days at
a time, but nobody took us seriously. When eventually we found this,
it was only thanks to a stroke of luck. But it suited us ideally because
the previous owners had already done all the structural work, the
wiring and the plumbing, and had built a very nice extension that is
the kitchen. For three years after we bought it we sat on deckchairs

The floor is a crazy paving of massive original flags. The pale green paint running around the wall and across the doors at dado level was inspired by the interior of a shop in Paris. The red velvet cushions, red Capellini lamp and the red poppies of the framed photograph by Andy Small seem to radiate warmth in a room dominated by the neutral tones of wood and stone.

The kitchen is a new extension at the back of the cottage, floored using reclaimed flags. The cupboard on the right came from an old draper's shop, the butcher's block provides a giant chopping board and the slate work surface and porcelain drainer next to the sink are also reclaimed. The enormous saucer ceiling lamps are from the Conran Shop.

and made do with a dishwasher and some bedrolls. An anonymous neighbour deposited a big bag of curtains on the doorstep, obviously concerned for our privacy. We didn't use them, but I did peg up some sheets of handmade paper on wires, which have been there ever since.'

Gradually Cressida and Chiara accumulated furniture. Some things were presents, others inherited and some they bought specially for the house. 'We wanted things that are robust, things we wouldn't have to worry about,' says Cressida. The result is an intriguing mix of the antique and the modern, the hip and the homely, in an interior that although fully restored has lost none of its sense of history.

The main body of the house probably dates from the 17th century, possibly earlier. In the 19th century, two more rooms upstairs and downstairs were added at the back and most recently the new kitchen was built, also at the back of the house. The original front door faces the garden, but today visitors come through a back door into the Victorian addition, now a spare room to the right of the narrow entrance hall, with a cloakroom and shower opposite. The oldest part of the house must once have been divided into two rooms and a hall, but a partition wall has been removed so that the staircase hall and living room are a single space. On the other side of the staircase is an informal dining room, which opens straight into the new kitchen.

Stone and wood give these rooms intrinsic character. The living room and dining room both have hefty stone fireplaces, one recently reconstructed, the other completely original. A crazy paving of giant

ABOVE LEFT One of Cressida's collection of old walking sticks hangs above the chopping board suspended from beams, the butcher's hooks looped over it holding a small selection of utensils, including a particularly rustic pair of salad servers. The pottery bowl with the plate of apples on top is an 'eco-cooler', made by Cressida's new company DeWeNe, and revives an old-fashioned way of storing root vegetables and fruit, which are kept cool by the evaporation of water soaked up by the pot from the plate it stands on. A piece of handmade paper clipped on a wire at the window screens the room from the lane.

ABOVE RIGHT Shelves beneath the sink and running under the slate work surface are protected by curtains made from sacking, a novel twist on a traditional idea. The glass bottles collected on the windowsill are round-bottomed flasks more often seen in a laboratory. A strip light along the back of the work surface illuminates the storage jars with an eerie glow.

stone slabs zigzags its way across the floor of the dining room, while new elm boards have been installed in the living room. The staircase, which must once have been boxed in, has had its underbelly of unfinished, worm-eaten wood exposed, its riven, creased texture contrasting with the youthful smoothness of the floor from which it rises. The original elm door to the downstairs bedroom has had no less than five keyholes punched through its venerable planks over the centuries, and upstairs there are old screen walls of broad, undulating elm boards, which have been stripped back to their warm, honey-coloured grain in the main bedroom.

This texture and patina of age makes an atmospheric setting for Cressida and Chiara's choice of furnishing, whether a sharp Ligne Roset bed in a spare room, or the towering white toadstool of the Cappellini lamp or the Matthew Hilton armchair in the living room. In the kitchen, which is the only room where the lines are straight and the plaster smooth, there is an imaginative mix of old fittings, which amply compensates for any loss of architectural character; a mahogany set of drawers and glass-fronted cupboards from an

The main bedroom has a wall of old and very wide elm planks, stripped back to the bare wood that is the colour of pale honey. On either side of the bed are two 'Airswitch' lamps by Mathmos, which are controlled by waving your hand in the air across their tops. The silk embroidered curtains and cushions are made in fabric from India.

Edwardian draper's shop makes practical storage, an enormous butcher's block provides a capacious work surface and curtains cut from old sacking cover the shelves under the long, slate work surface and butler's sink, both also antique.

The couple seem to specialize in decorative lateral thinking. Cressida collects sticks and has found a variety of uses for them, including curtain rods and rails for suspending kitchen implements. Logs are stored in old washing coppers, the downstairs bedroom has a wall sprinkled with wooden printing blocks, while white porcelain crucibles, round-bottomed flasks and fractional distillation bottles, more often seen in school laboratories, are decoratively displayed on some of the deep windowsills. 'I just really like the look of them,' Cressida says.

This ability to see and use things in a different context is perhaps part of Cressida's talent. Some of the Mathmos designs, several of which have found a place in the house, barely look like lights at all, and she has just started a new company called DeWeNe, which, among other unpretentious and useful products, has reinvented the shopping trolley as a smart series of hooks on wheels. 'We are making everything in Wales, as part of a social project,' Cressida elaborates. Creative thinking at its best.

FAR LEFT This downstairs spare bedroom is in the 'new' extension at the back of the house, built in the 19th century. Sprinkled across the wall behind the bed are wooden printing blocks carved with letters of the alphabet. More of them are lined up on the mantelpiece opposite the bed and the alphabet theme of the room is continued by a group of stones on the windowsill, each carved with a different letter.

BELOW LEFT Another of Cressida's collection of antique walking sticks is propped next to the door in an upstairs spare bedroom. None of the bedrooms have wardrobes, just hooks for hanging clothes on the wall.

ABOVE The star lights that illuminate the bathroom were bought in Morocco and the basin is antique French. Reflected in the mirror is another mirror made from an art deco electric fire surround.

BELOW AND FAR RIGHT The ground-floor dining room looks out over the churchyard and, like all the rooms in this elegantly modest house, appears not to have changed since the house was built. In fact, Stephen Pardy has moved its doorway, fitted a period hob grate and installed a period glazed cupboard where there was once a door to the kitchen. The 18th-century oak drop-leaf table and Windsor chairs stand on a rush mat by Felicity Irons.

RIGHT The principal windows of the house look south-west over a beautiful church close towards the 15th-century steeple and, beyond it, the Tudor red brick Deanery Tower. 'This is a house where the setting makes considerable demands on the design in order to do it justice,' says owner Stephen Pardy. The front facade was built using more expensive yellow brick, while the elevation facing the churchyard has to make do with less prestigious red brick.

RESTRAINED RETREAT

'This is a place for relaxation, entertaining and the pursuit of peace,' says Stephen Pardy of his early Victorian house in a small country town in Suffolk. The house was built in 1837 at the far end of a quiet side road named after the new Queen, whose coronation took place in the same year it was built.

Its proportions are modest, its style country Georgian and its three floors of sash windows look out over the trees and ancient tombstones of a grassy churchyard towards a 15th-century, lead-clad steeple and the Tudor brickwork of the Deanery Tower. It is this serene view that most appealed about the house when Stephen and his wife Clare decided to buy it as a country retreat three years ago.

The main facade of the house is yellow brick, while the end wall, which faces the churchyard, is in red brick. What now appears a charming quirk

Next to the dining room, the kitchen
also has a view of the church and
ancient tombstones. Stephen Pardy
designed the simple, robust cupboards
and drawers with their beech worktop
and open beech or zinc shelves above.
Opposite them there is a range cooker
in a white-tiled alcove flanked by period
storage cupboards. The top shelf above
the work surface carries a collection of
large, 19th-century slipware bowls.

was originally an act of architectural snobbery. Stephen Pardy explains that yellow brick was more expensive and therefore more prestigious at the beginning of the 19th century, so money was saved by using red brick round the corner where visitors arriving at the front door might not notice.

The house was originally twice as big, but was divided probably in the 19th century. What remains of the interior is the pretty staircase of steep, wooden treads and plain banisters, and two rooms on each floor, plus a top-floor bathroom and ground-floor cloakroom. Extra and invaluable space is provided by a one-room cellar fitted with racks for wine, logs and household supplies, and a wash house containing the boiler, washing machine, a sink and a workbench – 'All essential items,' as Stephen says, 'but ones that take up a lot of space and can cause mayhem if allowed to impinge.'

Achieving a sense of calm in this unassuming series of rooms has been Stephen Pardy's guiding principle. As a furniture and interiors designer, he

is acutely aware of the relationships between line, proportion, symmetry and colour, and the disturbing, almost emotional effect it can have when these relationships are ill-judged. 'Most of the changes I have made here have been a question of correcting mistakes,' he explains. Such is his skill that the corrections are invisible. The house feels and looks right, as if it has not been tampered with since the day the last coat of lead paint was brushed onto the glazing bars.

LEFT A view from the landing through to the drawing room and into the study. Stephen has chosen a limited and consistent palette of three colours throughout the house: a pale ivory for woodwork and ceilings, 'Trilby' by Dulux for floorboards and cupboard interiors and Dulux 'Flake Grey' for the walls. This, he says, helps to make 'rooms flow into one another as specific spaces within a unified whole', making the house seem more spacious.

ABOVE Beneath the kitchen window there is a zinc-topped preparation table, an ideal place to chop vegetables while enjoying the view. Stephen Pardy was determined to avoid the usual pitfalls of a second home with second-rate equipment and has made 'a really well thought-out batterie de cuisine' a priority. The long strips of wood painted with numbers are antique Swedish number boards, once used as a teaching aid in schools.

ABOVE LEFT Stephen's study is on the first floor, the William IV mahogany writing table that he uses as a desk strategically placed in the window with its stunning view of the fiercely pointed church steeple. The vintage anglepoise lamp and telephone have a reassuringly solid feel.

ABOVE RIGHT Also in the study Stephen has installed four sets of bookshelves, two on either side of the fireplace and two on the opposite wall. One of these was original, and taken from the drawing room, requiring a resizing of the study chimney breast in order to make it fit. Stephen's precise eye for proportion and design are apparent in the poised arrangement of objects, pictures, books and magazines.

A tour of the house armed with Stephen's immaculate before and after plans, and guided by his commentary, proves how wrong that initial impression is. Doors have been moved, other doors blocked in; chimney breasts have been widened; original cupboards have been copied and also resited; recent fitted cupboards have been removed; fireplaces have been installed. The layouts of the bathroom and cloakroom have been changed and walls subtly realigned to suit.

The first-floor drawing room is a good example of how apparently minor spatial adjustments can improve the feel of a room. Here, Stephen has widened the chimney breast in order to centralize the fire surround and has partially reinstated the wall that once separated the room from a room now lost to the house next door. This has created an entrance area with a small table under the side window, 'My Jane Austen desk,' Clare quips. A large mirror hangs exactly opposite the window at the far end of the main room, reflecting the light and the view. A wide opening, again centralized, links the two parts of the room. 'The important thing here,' explains Stephen, 'was to create a sense of symmetry and to line up the axis between the fireplace and the wall opposite, and the mirror and the window. These are refinements that you are not necessarily conscious of, but they make a space seem calm because the eye is satisfied.'

Stephen Pardy reveals that his other 'main trick' is to use a very limited colour palette to make rooms flow one into the other and to unify the interior so that the house seems more spacious than it actually is. 'In fact, only three paint colours have been used in the whole house,' he says. 'All the woodwork and ceilings are a very pale ivory. The floors,

The bookshelves opposite the fireplace in the study create an alcove into which fits another Stephen Pardy design, an ottoman daybed loosely based on a design by Gerrit Rietveld, upholstered in the same sacking used for prison mail sacks, its rough texture in appealing contrast to the grey and blue velvet cushions. The evocative photograph of a Norfolk farmer and his tractor is by Justin Partyka, and the Kazak rug is modern.

HERE AND RIGHT Stephen has worked hard to achieve symmetry in the drawing room, realigning the chimney breast and reinstating part of an original dividing wall to make a wide, architrave-framed opening opposite the window. On the other side of this opening, the mirror reflects the light and the view from the window. The result is a room that feels calm. The stools and pair of armchairs are Stephen's designs.

if not stone, are wide boards painted a period ginger brown, as are the cupboard interiors. All the walls are painted a pale, yellowish grey, a strange colour that makes an empty room resemble an experiment in sensory deprivation, but also has the invaluable quality of making anything put against it simply glow.'

It is true that the pictures and furnishings look particularly handsome, but this is not simply due to a well-chosen paint colour. Stephen's demanding eye has ensured that the contents of the house are as carefully edited as the rooms themselves have been organized and decorated. Much of the furniture, the armchairs, sofa and footstools in the drawing room, the daybed in the first-floor study and the plain wooden bedstead in the main bedroom at the top of the house are Stephen Pardy designs, elegant and comfortable. There are also antiques: an 18th-century oak table and Windsor chairs in the dining room, a 17th-century oak chest and a Pembroke table in the drawing room; restrained, country pieces that are perfectly at home in this restrained, country setting.

Clare works in art insurance and shares with Stephen a taste for Modern British drawings, prints, photography and sculpture. The wall opposite the fireplace in the drawing room is brought alive by powerful pencil sketches of a hare, preparatory drawings for a sculpture by Emma Stothard. 'Hares are a bit of a theme. I love them,' says Clare. A favourite is the alabaster hare, commissioned from sculptor Jude Taylor, which seems to hum with gathered light on the landing windowsill. Downstairs, works by Bridget Riley, Bill Brandt, Andy Warhol and Henry Moore hang in the ground-floor dining room, and there are black and white 20th-century photographs on the walls of the two landings.

'We were determined to avoid the usual drawbacks of second homes,' says Stephen, who is as articulate on the subject of the contents of the house as he is on its interior architecture. 'We didn't want to fill it with an accretion of unwanted, ill-matched furniture or have drawers full of blunt and broken kitchen utensils. We wanted peace, comfort and a really well thought-out batterie de cuisine.'

ABOVE RIGHT The top floor consists of a wide landing, two bedrooms and a bathroom. The guest bedroom with its white painted bed has 'proper sheets and blankets' and looks straight out to the church clock and its ancient sanctus bell that strikes the hours.

BELOW Stephen has managed to increase the bathroom floor space by realigning the walls and placing washbasin and lavatory on the same wall. The picture of a boat is made by the same technique used for rag rugs.

UNFINISHED BUSINESS

Katie Fontana's kitchen is not a good advertisement for her business. Not that it lacks beauty. In fact, it is more than beautiful. It is a kitchen with character; soul even, if a kitchen can be said to have such a thing. What it doesn't have is a single fitted cupboard or wall unit, or even so much as a cutlery drawer. 'Well, it does have a cherry wood prep table with a lovely zinc top,' Katie points out.

LEFT The kitchen is a long, narrow room that runs along the back of the house and is extremely simply furnished. The cherry wood 'prep table' with its zinc top and the cherry wood shelf above were made for the room by the kitchen company Plain English, which Katie Fontana founded in the early 1990s. A door at the far end of the room opens into a passage between the pub yard behind the house and the pedestrian alley at the front.

TOP RIGHT The window inside the hall was glazed in tin when Katie bought the house and was probably a serving hatch dating from the days when the house was a pub. In 1900 the room it looks into became a barber's shop and is now Katie's dining room.

RIGHT Katie found the 1.2-m (4-ft) wide stoneware sink on a pavement in Hoxton. The pictures propped on the shelf have a nautical theme (Katie and her partner are currently restoring a 1920s yacht in Cornwall) and include this engraving by John Weston of a clinker-built barge.

Opposite the prep table is an Aga, installed in the recess where there would have been a range. The old planked wall behind the fridge was directly in front of a later brick wall dividing the house from the building next door. Katie had it carefully moved forwards a couple of feet to make space for a capacious larder.

The food preparation table was made by the kitchen company Plain English, which Katie Fontana founded with partner Tony Niblock in the early '90s. 'The business began because we were building a house in Suffolk and couldn't find a kitchen we liked. The only one that appealed was a Shaker kitchen, but we could barely afford three cupboards. So, I designed one myself and had it made by local joiners,' Katie explains. The house was featured in a magazine and enquiries about where to buy the kitchen began to come in, so Katie and Tony decided to see if they could make a living designing and selling kitchens. Plain English has grown to compete with the big names in kitchen design, the traditional elegance of their range a welcome relief from the high-fashion fads of kitchen couture.

The house that Tony and Katie built, complete with Katie's first kitchen, was sold ten years ago, when Katie bought the house she now lives in. 'I bought it for two reasons,' Katie says. 'Because it was condemned, derelict and very cheap, but also because it hadn't been touched for 40 years, which was when it was last inhabited. Ever since it had been used as a store for the pub next door. They kept rabbits in the kitchen and there were no proper services; just an old lead water pipe and the remains of some silk-covered wiring. It had a fantastic atmosphere. What I didn't like was its location in the middle of a town. But it's only a little town and now I rather enjoy the convenience.'

TOP RIGHT A trio of antique metal lanterns sits in front of the old brick oven. On the right is a Victorian knife grinder used for polishing stainless steel knives.

RIGHT The cellar with its original brick alcoves dates from the 18th century when the building was a brewhouse for the pub next door. This and the ground floor are the oldest parts of the house.

LEFT AND ABOVE The dining room at the front of the house is a step up from the kitchen. The steps on the right lead down into the cellar. Ahead, Victorian candlesticks stand on a square piano dated 1826. Next to the bust on the windowsill is an antique rat cage, complete with sleeping house and exercise wheel. A piece of antique linen held up on bulldog clips affords privacy.

On a pedestrian alley, with the churchyard at one end and sandwiched between a pub and a Chinese restaurant, the house presents a rational facade of red brick and sash windows that gives little clue to its quaint and rustic interior. The rooms of the house seem to ramble as one leads into another, up steps, down stairs and round corners. The unusual layout is partly due to the different periods of building and partly to the way that the house has been divided from its neighbour, and is made more intriguing by the fact that behind closed doors some rooms are still 'building sites' and not yet in use.

The oldest parts of the house are the ground floor and the cellar, which were built as a brewhouse in the 18th century. In 1832 the publican went bankrupt and sold the property to a builder, who extended it and opened it as another pub with cheap lodgings above for visitors arriving on the new railway. Initials carved in some of the bricks on the facade may commemorate local traders who donated money to the enterprise.

Inside the narrow hall there is an internal window on the right that was glazed in tin, now exchanged for glass, and that

Katie thinks was probably a serving hatch. In 1900, when the pub closed, the room behind the window became a barber's shop. Today it is Katie's dining room. A door at the back and a step down take you into the kitchen; a long, narrow room of striking simplicity running across the back of the house. The floor is brick and the walls are also brick painted white. There is a shiny black Aga set into a recess where there must once have been a range and directly opposite it there is the prep table. The two windows look out onto the yard at the back of the pub, but there is no view of stacked metal barrels or beer crates because the windows are glazed with Victorian holophane glass, an ingenious invention originally used to magnify the light from oil lamps. Here it serves the double function of providing extra light, plus privacy, as it is translucent rather than transparent. Beneath one of the windows is a wide, shallow stoneware sink.

Aside from the Aga and the large retro fridge, the kitchen seems barely touched by the 21st century. The light slanting through the windows onto the worn brick floor, the sink and the lack of gadgets give the room the plain, old-fashioned

The original fireplace in the dining room had been boarded up and the register grate had rusted. Katie found another that fitted exactly at a reclamation yard. The walls are painted in Farrow & Ball 'Wall White' and antique Suffolk ball and bar chairs are set around a Georgian drop-leaf table. The chandelier is French.

The sitting room is on the first floor and next to a landing large enough for a grand piano. The antique sofa is upholstered in grey velvet. The fire surround, which Katie started stripping, is only propped and the pretty Georgian armchair has been stripped of its later upholstery. In the foreground are two worn Sheffield plate candlesticks and a Wedgwood jug.

feel of a 17th-century Dutch interior. This is testament to the care with which Katie restored and furnished it. 'A fully-fitted kitchen never felt quite appropriate,' she says. Structural alterations included taking down a wall that divided the space into two rooms and moving the planked wall, directly behind which was a later brick wall, a couple of feet forwards into the room to create a larder. The brick floor was taken up so that insulation could be laid beneath it and then re-laid, ensuring that broken bricks were not separated and that the most worn bricks were put in the middle.

The sink was found by Katie on the pavement in Hoxton outside the Plain English showroom, which was in the process of being fitted out. 'I talked to the builders who had dumped it and they said I could have it if I could take it away. Fortunately, I had my own builders on hand to help me.' Hidden beneath the sink is one of Katie's few and discreet modern luxuries, a water softener, and next to it, masked by a wooden door, there is a dishwasher.

Both dining room and kitchen are finished, but a door on the other side of the Aga leads into one of several unrestored rooms in the house. When she gets round to clearing and decorating it, this will be the breakfast room. From here, a staircase will lead up to three further rooms for use as a study, a spare bedroom and bathroom. At the top of the hall stairs another closed door marks a room destined to be 'a beautiful, big bathroom'. Up again and there is a second generous landing, with a small shower room tucked in next to the stairs. A further mini flight of stairs takes you up to Katie's bedroom.

Katie is in no particular rush to get the house finished. 'It's just how I am,' she laughs. 'The first thing I do is rip out everything I don't like and then I can picture what it will be like when it's done, at which point I feel quite content. Also, I know myself well enough to recognize that, once everything is complete, I will get the urge to move on. And I do have a fear of over-restoring and losing the character that made me love the house when I first saw it.'

ABOVE Like the floor below, the third floor has a generous landing where Katie has a desk. The mini staircase on the left leads up to her bedroom. The different floor levels and low ceilings give the house a quaint, cottagey feel.

RIGHT The shower room was a complete surprise; an unclaimed, empty space full of cobwebs between Katie's landing and a bathroom in the pub next door that was discovered only when the ceiling below was taken down. A plastic hoop from Toys R Us supports the shower curtain.

Katie bought her bed from an antique shop in Nice with the intention of re-upholstering it, but has never got round to doing it. The bedside table is a Georgian pot cupboard. The fireplace had been boarded up and the original register grate had rusted, but Katie found an identical one to replace it. Shelves hold towels and linen.

Over-restoration is something Katie could never be accused of. She has carefully preserved every door, every floorboard, every brick, every wooden wall complete with patina and imperfections. As for leaving things unfinished, quite aside from the rooms still requiring attention, there are projects dotted all over the house, from the 'trick' fire surround propped up in the living room that shifts if leant upon, to the Georgian armchair next to it that has been stripped back to its patched underwear, and the curtain in Katie's bedroom that remains hanging loosely on the same piece of braid she hurriedly tacked up in honour of a visit from her mother. She might modestly blame these decorative omissions on a habit of prevarication, but they are very much part of the appeal of the peaceful, pretty rooms that she has gently coaxed back to life. And it doesn't seem likely she will feel the need to move any time soon.

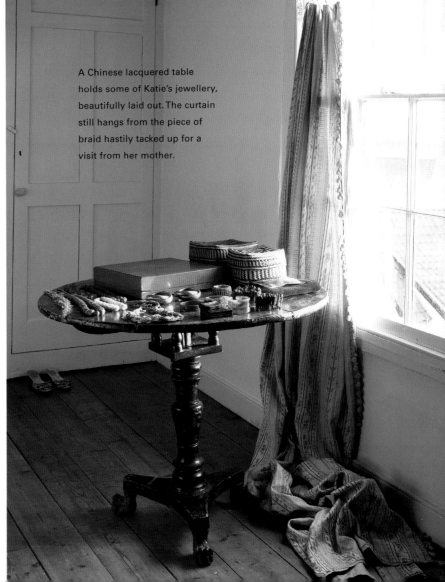

A Chinese lacquered table holds some of Katie's jewellery, beautifully laid out. The curtain still hangs from the piece of braid hastily tacked up for a visit from her mother.

TOP RIGHT To the right of the window opposite Katie's bed is a Regency chest of drawers, which she bought from an Essex antique shop. Getting it up the stairs was made easier by the fact that it had already been cut in half for exactly the same reason. The Victorian print propped on top shows scenes from a circus, including a cat doing a handstand on a horse. The sofa, like the bed, is French.

SIMPLICITY
finishing touches

• FURNITURE The antique country furniture that Hall & Hirschhorn specialize in is as expensive as it is desirable. More affordable alternatives include unpretentious and utilitarian, mass-produced furnishings from the last century, such as chapel chairs and the 1950s folding school chairs that Cressida Granger keeps stacked against the wall when not in use.

• BESPOKE A more straightforward piece of furniture, such as a table, can be commissioned from a local joiner. This may be an opportunity to recycle old wood, like the reclaimed floorboards that form the top of Cressida Granger's extra-long table.

• BASKETS A country craft that continues to flourish is basket making, especially in areas such as the Somerset Levels where willow is still grown commercially. Baskets are handsome and multi-functional, useful for storing logs, toys, vegetables, lavatory roll or laundry, as well as for housing dogs and babies.

• WINDOWS Curtains can look too lavish for this pared-down style. Stephen Pardy uses discreet, cream roller blinds, barely visible when not in use. Internal folding shutters are a good alternative and can be made to fit if you are not lucky enough to have old ones in working order.

• FLOORING Traditional floorings in stone, wood, brick or clay tiles have the right natural feel. Soften them with seagrass or sisal mats, bound at the edges, as in Stephen Pardy's house.

• KITCHENS Sometimes a fitted kitchen is the best use of space, but if you have the luxury of a larger room, consider visiting architectural salvage dealers for old shop fittings or a butcher's block for extra work surface, both features of Cressida Granger's kitchen.

• CURTAINS These are an attractive and old-fashioned way to protect under-counter kitchen shelves from dust, and much less expensive than hinged doors. Cressida Granger has used sacking, which looks interestingly modern. A striped, checked or sprigged cotton would be more traditional.

• WARDROBES Fitted wardrobes, like fitted kitchens, can look wrong in a small cottage bedroom. Antique cupboards are usually too shallow for coat hangers, as, until the late 19th century, clothes were either stored flat in chests and drawers or hung on hooks. The bedrooms in Cressida Granger's cottage are delightfully wardrobe-free, although all have wall hooks where clothes can be temporarily hung. Instead, she has devoted a box room to clothes storage. Even without the benefit of a box room, you might consider confining fitted wardrobes to a secondary bedroom in order to leave at least one bedroom unobstructed.

ELEGANCE

THE ELEVATION OF THE COTTAGE FROM
IMPOVERISHED HOVEL TO DESIRABLE HOME IS
A RELATIVELY RECENT PHENOMENON. WHEN
COLERIDGE AND SOUTHEY WERE WRITING
THEIR SATIRICAL COUPLETS, THEIR CRITICISM
WAS AIMED AT THE PRETENSIONS OF WEALTHY
SOPHISTICATES MASQUERADING AS SIMPLE
COUNTRY FOLK. TODAY THERE IS NOTHING
CONTRADICTORY ABOUT COMFORT,
SOPHISTICATION OR WEALTH RESIDING IN A
COTTAGE, NOR NEED A COTTAGE INTERIOR BE
ANY LESS ELEGANT THAN THAT OF A RAMBLING
RECTORY OR LOFTY TOWN HOUSE. SMALL
AND BEAUTIFUL, THE INTERIORS ON THE
FOLLOWING PAGES PROVE THE POINT.

ARTIST IN RESIDENCE

*'This is me,' says Binny Mathews, running her hand across the top of
a chair back, 'and this is Stuart,' running her hand over its seat. The
chair is a cross between a traditional hall chair and a modern dining chair.
It is pulled up to a kitchen table that is littered with tubes of paint.
'I have just been painting the dining room candles green,' says Binny.
'Oil paint sticks extremely well to wax – there really is no need to
buy coloured candles when you can make them yourself.'*

ABOVE Binny Mathews and Stuart
Martin first spotted the secluded
farmhouse that is now their home while
admiring a panoramic view of some of
the Dorset countryside immortalized by
Thomas Hardy. Throughout the summer
months the cottage garden is adorned by
a tented pavilion designed by Stuart and
made by Bennett's Marquees of Poole.

Binny Mathews' skill with a paintbrush is more often applied to canvas. She is a
portrait painter of renown, with paintings in the collections of The National Trust,
HRH The Prince of Wales and the American Embassy in London. Her husband,
Stuart Martin, is an architect whose practice specializes in conservation and the
building of new country houses in a traditional mould. The chair we have been
discussing was a collaboration between Binny and Stuart, and the two in the

LEFT Entering through the original
front door (now the back door that
leads into the garden), the living room
is on your right. When Binny and Stuart
first moved in, the huge fireplace had
been partially bricked up. After opening
it out again, they had to install a high
brick plinth to prevent it from smoking.
A double portrait by Binny hangs above
the knole sofa and the ceramic table
lamp is by potter Seth Cardew.

RIGHT In a corner of the same
room a portrait of Stuart by Binny
hangs above a painted bridal chest
from Hydra. The warm, earthy yellow
of the walls is the result of artistic
experiment. The still life on the
right-hand wall is also by Binny.

RIGHT AND BELOW The glamorous dining room was previously a kitchen with Formica on the ceiling and patched lino on the floor. Binny has painted the walls a deep, midnight blue, which makes a dramatic foil to the antique furnishings, including a table from Talisman and a tapestry from Joanna Booth. The dining chairs are the result of a design collaboration between Stuart and Binny and are veneered in dark walnut. The pottery plates are by Seth Cardew.

FAR RIGHT Binny's 'office' opposite the living room has the feminine charm of a boudoir and is furnished with almost rococo frivolity. A pair of French painted chairs flanks the fireplace and the mantelpiece has a chinoiserie feel with its arrangement of oriental porcelain. The painting between the wall sconces is a Tuscan landscape by Binny.

kitchen are prototypes. A set of them in laminated walnut is placed around the antique dining table. 'They had to be made specially because the table is unusually high. I think it may have been a side table,' says Binny, 'but it was the perfect, long, slim shape for the room.'

A dining room may seem an unusual luxury in a cottage, but when Binny and Stuart first moved in 12 years ago, it was a kitchen and the kitchen was a tractor store, its window shutters nailed shut, its beautiful stone floor hidden under a layer of compacted mud and engine oil. The house is at least 300 years old and was built as a farmhouse. Its symmetrical front looks out over woodland and fields. On either side of a central hall leading from front to back of the house are two reception rooms, one of which Binny uses

as an office. The narrow room that runs along the back of the house and is now the dining room is a later addition, as is the kitchen also at the back of the house. Upstairs there are four rooms above the reception rooms, a bedroom each for their school-age sons Rufus and Quentin, a main bedroom and a dressing room, and above the kitchen, there is a sizeable bathroom. Like the kitchen, this is reclaimed space, formerly uninhabitable.

Binny's instructions on how to find the house include the sentence 'You will know when you are nearly there because there is the most wonderful view'. Just as she promises, the lane that leads to the house and to another farm, and to nowhere else, rounds a bend between trees and fields and suddenly presents you with a wide panorama of smooth, green hills patched with darker woodland, fading to shades of grey and violet as it meets the distant horizon. 'We lived in a cottage in the next village and we used to drive here and sit looking at that view,' says Binny. 'You could see the roof of this house below, among trees, but it had a mysterious aura of privacy, so we never went further down the lane to look at it. Then we heard that the old boy who lived here, who was 90 and nearly blind,

needed to move and we offered to swap houses. We came here and he stayed in our cottage until he died.'

The old man had lived in primitive conditions, cutting his own wood and tipping the contents of the outdoor lavatory over his vegetable garden. The utility room next to the kitchen was dominated by a wood-burning boiler that had to be stoked once or twice through the night to keep it going

LEFT The colour of the walls in the office is hard to pin down, a pale, aqueous shade somewhere between green and blue. Sadly, it is not available from a pot, as it is the result of many layers of paint and glaze built up by Binny until she achieved the precise effect she wanted. Hanging against it, and reflecting light from the window, is a grand pair of Italian mirrors topped by 'big, fat cherubs'. Binny's desk can be seen in the reflection.

RIGHT Binny bought the French sofa, which still has its original Aubusson upholstery, from a friend. The Continental sophistication of the furnishings in this room is in contrast to the more robust, English style of the living room. The flooring in both rooms is coir matting, which has the right rustic feel for a cottage interior, but laid wall to wall looks equally appropriate as a background to more refined furnishings. Pictures are a mix of works by Binny herself, by friends and by unknown artists.

and that took a week to warm the house from when first lit. Soon after they moved in, Binny and Stuart began the filthy if satisfying work of unearthing original features: ripping the Formica off the ceiling of the old kitchen to reveal limewashed boarding, taking up the lino that was smothering the flags and excavating a broad, high farmhouse fireplace that had been filled in with breeze blocks in the living room.

There are also boarded ceilings in the new kitchen and the bathroom, attractively mottled with the remains of old limewash. Only in the dining room did they painstakingly scrape off the old paint in order to apply a new coat. 'It

didn't seem a very good idea to have little white flakes dropping into the soup,' says Binny, pragmatically.

The house has an untouched feel, as though it has been gently ageing without interruption. This is partly because of Binny and Stuart's decisions to leave well alone where practical, but is also due to the care expended on additions and changes. Binny says that she approaches the decoration and furnishing of each room as she does a painting. One result of her artistic eye is that the final colour of every wall has been arrived at as a result of experiment and layering, in much the same way as you might build colour on a canvas.

LEFT Above a birdcage on the kitchen windowsill, Binny has painted a selection of garden birds directly onto the wall. 'Every time one of the boys spotted a new species, I painted it,' she explains. 'But I am afraid I gave up when they saw a pheasant.' The marble slab was found in the garden and was probably the top of an old washstand.

BELOW Next to the kitchen table are two prototypes of the dining chairs designed by Stuart with input from Binny. The room had been used as a tractor shed and the old flags were found underneath a thick layer of mud and engine oil.

One of the most elegant rooms is Binny's office. Filling the wall opposite the fireplace is a French 18th-century sofa, still dressed in its faded Aubusson, and opposite the window hangs a pair of Italian gilt mirrors, topped by plump cherubs. There are gilded sconces over the fireplace, Chinese porcelain plates and a painted pelmet, from which float white muslin curtains. The effect is soft, feminine and delicate. The furniture looks as though it could have sat here for generations and the evasive colour of the walls, a shade somewhere between sage green and duck egg blue, has a depth and patina that looks equally antique. In fact, it is all Binny's work, starting with three coats of eggshell blue, then a thin coat of green that was too bright, followed by a thin coat of a softer green and lastly a glaze of matt varnish.

The drawing room is a dirty, mustard yellow, the result of similar layering, and the dining room is dusky midnight blue. It is a theatrical backdrop for the panel of tapestry, the candle sconces and the mirror; but Binny chose it in order to make the walls disappear at night. 'When you are gathered around the table to eat, the occasion should be all about conversation. The dark walls help focus energy, so you are not distracted by your surroundings.'

Binny's explanation of the kitchen is similarly forthright, and unexpected. 'I really can't see the point of fitted kitchens,' she says. 'If you need a surface, put one in. If you need a cupboard, fix one up. But there's no need to follow the crowd.' Binny's work surface is a long, pine shelf on brackets under the window on the wall opposite the door. The slab of marble placed on it was found in the garden. To the right, a Georgian mahogany corner cupboard houses spices and jars. At right angles to the work surface, underneath a second window, is a Belfast sink with a wooden surround and plain cupboards beneath designed by Stuart. Opposite the sink are a very large, stainless steel fridge and a stainless steel range cooker. 'That's the silver side,' says Binny gesturing towards the fridge, 'while the other side of the kitchen is white.' A careful balancing of colour that typifies her artistic approach.

Binny is vehemently against the idea of a fitted kitchen. The closest this room comes to being fitted is the Belfast sink under the window, which is mounted in a unit designed by Stuart. The recessed spotlight looks strikingly modern in its setting of mottled pine ceiling boards.

ABOVE LEFT Like the office below it, the main bedroom has a slightly Frenchified feel. Both rooms have ornate carved pelmets above their small casement windows and are dominated by French furniture. In this room, the sofa with its original velvet upholstery was bought at Lawrence's auction house in nearby Crewkerne. The antique bed has been cunningly widened to bring it into line with the dimensions of a modern double bed.

ABOVE The spectacularly large bathroom is directly above the kitchen and was used as an attic space, except for the lavatory to the left of this window, which was walled off as a separate room. The space and light are magnified by the all-white colour scheme, which includes the old limewash still adhering to the boarded ceiling. A giant clamshell sits on one of the windowsills.

LEFT Paintings next to the bed are a mix of works by Binny and friends, including James Hart Dyke, Julian Bailey, Arthur Neal and Tia Lambert.

The bathroom was originally in the room next door to this, a space now used as a capacious walk-in-and-around wardrobe. They kept the old cast-iron roll-top bathtub and placed it in the centre of the new bathroom. Capacious baskets hold clean linen and a spiky aloe vera plant crowns the cupboard.

IN THE PINK

Antique dealers Doris Urquhart and Christopher Richardson bought their tall, thin Regency house in the middle of a small Sussex town because they couldn't resist it. 'We were living in a village not far from here, and we already knew the house when it came up for sale,' Doris explains. 'With its doll's house proportions and those little round holly trees by the doors, it has that covetable quality of a wonderful artefact — something you would like to put on your mantelpiece and look at,' she smiles.

Doris Urquhart's style is more cottage than town house. She describes her taste as tending towards folk art and country simplicity, influenced by her American background. Christopher, who is English, favours more traditionally beautiful antiques. 'He would choose a lovely hand-painted porcelain plate, where I might prefer an earthenware colander.'

This house appealed to them both. From the outside it has a certain elegance, standing aloof like an upended shoebox, its symmetrical front dignified by the dark glitter of glazed 'mathematical' tiles that throw into relief the white paint of sash windows and arched doors. The formality is gently undermined by the slightly peculiar layout of the doors and windows. Despite the narrow frontage, there are two identical doors, each pushed to the furthest edges of the house: one a front door, the other a tradesman's entrance. Between these doors is a single window and above it are two slimmer, longer windows on the first floor. A second pair of much squatter windows peers out from under the eaves. It is as if someone had been given all the right architectural elements and then put them together in the wrong places.

LEFT The kitchen is on the raised ground floor at the back of the house where bay windows were added later in the 19th century. The view is of the leafy back garden and the ancient castle walls. Candles are lit for an evening dinner party.

ABOVE RIGHT The facade of the house is clad in glossy 'mathematical tiles', its perfect symmetry emphasized by the twin balls of the clipped bay trees. The door on the left opens into the hall, while the one on the right was originally for tradesmen.

ABOVE Doris and Christopher took up all the fitted carpets, exposing the original floorboards, here seen running from the hall into the kitchen. Interior woodwork, including the staircase, is much plainer than the ostentatious facade might suggest.

Behind this genteel if quirky facade, the interior of the house is surprisingly plain, the rooms cosy rather than gracious, and altogether a more suitable setting for Doris's style of furnishing than outward appearances might suggest. Christopher can enjoy the relative sophistication of the sitting room with its tall front windows that reach down to the floor, but the rest of the rooms have the feel of a cottage, albeit one on four floors with views over the high street at the front and a castle at the back.

According to local legend, the house was built by a prosperous butcher in order to house his mother. 'Mr and Mrs Butcher lived in the big house next door,' as Doris tells it. 'When Mr Butcher died and Master Butcher married, he wanted the big house to himself, so used

BELOW Doris has a weakness for antique doll's houses, but no desire to fill them with miniature furniture. Instead, she uses them as cupboards. Folded linen tea towels can be seen through the windows of this one in the kitchen.

ABOVE RIGHT Antique storage jars and antique bread boards are all in use in the kitchen where the only slice of modernity is the stainless steel gas cooker. As elsewhere in the house, all the woodwork is painted the same shade of pink.

a bit of his garden to make separate accommodation for Mummy Butcher. But we don't think he can have liked her very much. In order not to appear mean, he made sure the house looked good from the street, but inside the poor lady didn't have so much as a cornice to bless herself with. All the fireplaces are tiny and there is not one original architectural embellishment beyond the strictly necessary.'

Mrs Butcher may have felt short-changed, but 'It suits us very well,' says Doris. 'When an old friend of mine who is also an antique dealer first visited us here, she laughed because she said we had been extremely clever and somehow managed to combine two very disparate looks under one roof.' Doris disparagingly calls it a 'mishmash'. Certainly, the house contains an unusual mix that puts gilt next to gingham, rough country pottery beneath a Regency convex mirror and naive portraits opposite a sophisticated oil painting. 'I do like strange combinations,' says Doris, 'otherwise an interior can become very boring and formulaic.'

There is nothing boring about the contents of this house. Doris's country furniture rubs shoulders with Georgian and Regency mahogany and every room, landing, windowsill, shelf and mantelpiece is enlivened by interesting and unusual objects, artfully arranged and displayed. 'I would never describe myself as a collector in the scientific sense of the word,' says Doris, 'although as a child I did

By hanging a set of 18th-century oak shelves above a Victorian sideboard, Doris has created the effect of a kitchen dresser and the opportunity to display a fascinating selection of antiques, including mochaware jugs, decoy pigeons, butter moulds, a sovereign bank and a Napoleonic prisoner-of-war bone carving of a skeleton.

collect first editions of children's books. If I see something I really like I will often buy more than one, but I have to bump into it rather than undertaking an organized search.'

The results of frequent 'bumps' include a flock of English decoy pigeons that roost along the top of the kitchen shelves, a scattered hamlet of Victorian doll's houses that Doris likes to use as cupboards, for tea towels in the kitchen or toiletries in the bathroom, and a family of French papier mâché

milliner's heads, once used to display bonnets, whose solemn faces regard one another across the sitting room. In the same room, handsome blue and white Delft pottery fills the shelves of a Dutch marquetry cabinet, a piece of which came away at one point and was glued back on upside down, and back in the kitchen on the shelves beneath the decoy pigeons there is a bowl of dozens of china decoy eggs, gathered over the years, and a group of mochaware jugs.

The sitting room on the first floor is the grandest room in the house, although even this room had only a tiny fireplace originally. Doris describes the 18th-century Dutch marquetry cabinet as 'quite mad'. The pair of papier mâché heads are French, early 19th century and were made to display bonnets.

LEFT There are two more miniature houses on the top landing, this time in glass cases. Sitting on top are two Victorian peg dolls, while an antique Noah's ark forms part of the arrangement on the 18th-century chest. The fruit in the bowl is also antique. The curtains are plain cream linen.

BELOW AND OVERLEAF Christopher's study is on the first floor behind the living room. Here, as elsewhere, the flooring is the original boards, the Phillips screws that had been used to secure them replaced by old-fashioned nails. The Victorian button-back chair is upholstered in plain linen and above it hangs a group of 18th-century prints.

Although the rooms are not large or numerous – two bedrooms and a bathroom in the basement, a front room and kitchen on the ground floor, sitting room and study on the first floor and two more bedrooms and a bathroom at the top – and despite the wealth of contents, the house feels roomy and ordered. 'It seemed smaller when we bought it,' remembers Doris. 'The lady who owned it was extremely precise and particular. She skimmed all the old plaster to make the walls nice and straight, and had fitted turquoise carpets everywhere and a lot of furniture. We replaced her kitchen and bathrooms, using old fittings, and we took up all the carpet. We sanded the old boards and removed kilos of Phillips screws that had been used to secure them and replaced them with nails. As a result the floors give large squeaks in certain places, but I would rather that than have to live with hundreds of modern screws.'

Liberated from later accretions, the house immediately looked more spacious. Then, according to Doris, Christopher woke up one morning and announced that he thought the whole interior should be painted pink; 'Porphyry Pink' to be precise, a Farrow & Ball colour that Doris had used once before in her house in London. Although this soft terracotta is a traditional colour, described by the manufacturers as 'often used on walls as a foil to

The antique brass bed almost fills the bedroom and is placed with its head beneath one of the two windows, as the door and fireplace take up space on the other two walls. An antique patchwork quilt is laid over the duvet and the striped curtains have been lengthened to fit with a plain border.

LEFT When they bought the house, Doris and Christopher removed all later fittings, including in the kitchen and bathrooms. In this bathroom they have replaced them with an antique basin, a lavatory with an old wooden seat and an antique roll-top bathtub. The tiles behind the basin are 17th-century Delft and the framed cut-out silhouette pictures are early 19th century.

BELOW The miniature fireplace in the main bedroom can only have held a few lumps of coal and is prettily dwarfed by the antique spongeware jug on its mantel. A small group of early 20th-century soft toys huddles on the Regency armchair.

porphyry details such as columns during the Regency period', Doris and Christopher have not used it in a traditional manner. While the floors, stairs and banisters and some of the doors have been stripped to the wood, every other surface, including architraves, window frames, fitted cupboards, ceilings, skirting boards and shelving, is pink. The effect is of a uniform glow, a bit like being deep inside a conch shell. 'It's a very good trick if you want to create a plain, calm background for lots of stuff,' Doris explains. 'Although these rooms are nicely proportioned, there is nothing in the way of architectural detail worth picking out. Better to paint it all the same colour and let the eye flow over it.'

No interior as carefully arranged as this happens without sacrifice. Doris admits that they were forced to edit their possessions severely before they moved in. 'We sold so much, but I have to admit that we did keep some things we just couldn't bear to let go.' Behind the firmly closed door of one of the basement bedrooms is an uncharacteristic muddle of stacked furniture and boxes. 'It's not so much a store room as a very large, very full packing case,' Doris laughs. 'But perhaps one day we will move and find somewhere to put it all.'

HERE AND RIGHT The wide entrance hall, seen through the doorway, opens into the kitchen at one end of the long, one-storey building. The flooring, which looks like stone, is concrete paving slabs that have been tinted and coated with a semi-matt sealant. The shelving unit was made by George Carter for an exhibition at Christie's and the steel-topped table, shown right, is another of his 'cobbling togethers'. Chairs from the café at Uppark surround a pine table bought from 'a seedy shop in Lincolnshire'.

CARTER'S SHED

Award-winning garden and exhibition designer George Carter is also a master of illusion. He can create a baroque facade from painted plywood or a candelabrum from brass door plates. He can make MDF desirable and galvanized steel look like 18th-century mirror glass. He finds treasures on skips and insists he never spends money on anything. Yet his house and garden, his barns and even his outside lavatory are so handsome, so beautifully arranged, so pleasing from all angles that you would be inclined to disbelieve him if you didn't know better.

TOP RIGHT The front door with its pretty, gothic glazing was once the middle of one of three small arched windows when the building was an engine shed. The gate at the end of the garden path was inspired by an 18th-century painting.

ABOVE The robustly classical hall table was made to a design by George from painted and silvered wood, using silver leaf. Above it hangs a trio of mirrored sconces in a typically balanced composition, only the generous arrangement of flowers providing a dash of asymmetry.

LEFT The original arched windows have metal frames that do not open, but this casement window is new. The antique table and stool were bought 'very cheaply' in one of the circuit of local antique shops that George visits regularly, and the curtain material was from his favourite draper's shop.

HERE A pair of armchairs from IKEA forms part of a grouping of pairs, which includes the lamps, the glass obelisks and the potted ferns. The original arched window has been given a chunky wooden shutter.

On the edge of the grounds of George Carter's neat Norfolk farmhouse there is a long, low building constructed in the mid-19th century to house the steam engine for a mechanized threshing machine. He bought it from a local farmer and has converted it to make holiday and guest accommodation. And, in the same way that he can conjure the spirits of Vanbrugh and Kent in MDF, he has taken a humble engine shed and transformed it into a small masterpiece of classical restraint.

The single-storey building already had its good points. Constructed from flint, with red brick detailing and a roof of fox brown pantiles, its facade was pierced by three small, arched windows. 'There was something Italianate about its design,' George Carter says, 'and this suggested using a bold, vaguely classical style for the interior.' He enlarged the middle window to make a front door with pretty, gothic glazing bars, and to this perfectly symmetrical, satisfyingly simple central block he added an extension at both ends, one of which houses the drawing room, the other a utility room off the kitchen.

Inside the resulting three-bay bungalow, the layout has a bold originality. Instead of a small entrance hall with rooms leading off it, the front door opens straight into a long, deep room that stretches across two-thirds of the original engine shed. At either end of this wide corridor, generous openings unencumbered by doors give views

through to the drawing room on the right and the kitchen on the left. Ahead, behind planked doors, are the two bedrooms and shower rooms. Arguably, this arrangement is a needless waste of space in a relatively small house, but the luxury of a long vista from one end of the building to the other seems worth the sacrifice.

The architectural detailing, as George intended, is reminiscent of a Tuscan villa. The arched windows have chunky, planked shutters, the architraves around the doors are bold and plain and there is a weighty bolection moulding surrounding the drawing room fireplace. Adding to the sense of solidity, the floor is what appears to be polished stone. In fact, it is one of George's clever economies. 'It's concrete paving slabs that have been given a slight tint of colour to make them look a bit like Bath stone,' he admits. 'They're from a family firm in Fakenham and I like them even better used inside than out.'

Generosity of scale and decorative sleights of hand also inform the cottage furnishings, which have a rustic grandeur that is perfectly suited to their setting. Inevitably, George insists that 'most of the contents are characterized by having been bought very cheaply'. If you test him on individual items, you have to concede that this is true.

Picking on a smart antique upholstered stool in the window of the drawing room, he reveals that it cost £60. In the same room, the side tables and the armchairs are from IKEA, and the striped curtain fabric from 'an old-fashioned draper's shop in King's Lynn.' He is particularly pleased with the large, silver lamp bases, which he bought for £15 each from an ironmonger in Fakenham. The pine kitchen table from 'a seedy shop in Lincolnshire' is lifted from the ordinary to the interestingly austere by its slightly frivolous accompanying chairs, copied from an 18th-century version at Uppark and bought as a job lot from the café there when it was refurbished.

Beefing up the more conventional furnishings are items designed by George

FAR RIGHT The striped theme is continued in the bed linen. Hanging above the bed are two Victorian tinsel pictures of theatrical characters. George has a stock of old frames that he can cut down to fit and match up with his collection of unframed prints and pictures.

RIGHT In the same bedroom the chest at the end of the bed is 19th century, as is the spongeware bowl. A small Edwardian table and toilet mirror serve as a neat dressing table.

BOTTOM RIGHT The second bedroom is decorated with rows of George's watercolours from his book *Garden Spaces*. The frames are modern, but are given extra character by hanging them the old-fashioned way from a top-mounted hook.

Opposite the IKEA armchairs is an antique sofa that George bought from a friend, complete with its prettily scalloped, stripey loose cover. The silvered table lamps are another of George's bargains, bought for £15 each from a local ironmonger. The 17th-century prints above the sofa include two of the houses where George has worked on the gardens.

himself. These include a row of fat straw obelisks in the hall made for the Grosvenor House Antiques Fair and a robust side table with a silvered finish, also in the hall. Just beyond it, under the kitchen window, is another of George's creations, again a side table, but this time uncompromisingly modern in style. 'I put that together in about 1970,' George reveals. 'The legs started as part of a sculpture and the top is from a steel catering table. It was one of the thinnings that came out of the house.'

It is hardly surprising that, as well as designing gardens and exhibitions, George also works as an interior designer. He has worked on rooms at the American Museum and is currently busy on a Georgian house for which he is architect, garden designer and interior designer all in one.

Considering his love of illusion and ability to contrive grand effects on a low budget, it seems surprising that no one has asked him to work on theatre design. 'Yes, I would enjoy that,' he muses.

ABOVE From the back, William Thuillier thinks his flint folly, once an 18th-century bathhouse, looks like a toy fort. The double steps were added later, when the bathhouse became a dower house. Beneath the steps, a grotto-like tunnel leads to a door with access to the lower ground floor.

ABOVE RIGHT William had the front door copied from the door of an 18th-century house in *Country Life*. The steep staircase on the right was designed in gothic style by American interior decorator Robert Perkins.

GOTHIC FOLLY

'From one side it looks like a doll's house, from the other it looks like a toy fort.' William Thuillier's description of his Hampshire cottage makes it sound delightful, and the reality does not disappoint. Sitting on a grassy mound against a backdrop of trees, it has blue-painted gothic windows in a knobbly flint facade. Its doll's house front, overlooking fields, is decorated with pierced quatrefoils and stone medallions, while round the back there are ivy-draped steps leading up to the entrance with an arched tunnel below.

The diminutive reception rooms are each lit by a single gothic arched window and have been given extra grandeur by the raising of the ceilings and the addition of antique chimney pieces. The painting is of William's great-grandmother as a child and was cut off at the knees by her when older to hide her frilly knickerbockers.

ABOVE A view from one of the two
identical reception rooms that flank the
octagonal dining room, looking into
the inner hall and entrance hall beyond.
The 18th-century bookcase is one of
several pieces specially chosen for the
house for its gothic-influenced design.

RIGHT The central dining room is
one of the original 18th-century rooms
in the building and is directly above the
room that housed the plunge bath. The
small, octagonal dining table reflects
the unusual shape of the room, and
two gothic windows and a glazed door
overlook the fields that were once part
of the landscape gardens, possibly
designed by Capability Brown to make
a fashionable setting for the main
house. The chinoiserie wallpaper is
from de Gournay.

In this facade there are only two tiny windows, not much wider than arrowslits, flanking the door. The walls rise much higher than at the front because the land drops away, and this, just as William Thuillier suggests, gives the building the appearance of a miniature castle.

Visitors arriving along the curved, wooded drive get a glimpse of the doll's house but enter through the toy fort. At the top of the steps to the door you can see over the wall of the Victorian garden to the roof of a large new house and the tower of a Saxon church beyond. Church, wall, house and cottage represent different stages in the development of an estate that has seen as many owners over the centuries as it has changes in architectural fashion.

The cottage dates from the second half of the 18th century when the estate was bought by John de Burgh, 11th Earl of Clanricarde. Clanricarde lavished expense on his new property, transforming the grounds into fashionably romantic parkland. There is some evidence to suggest that he employed the landscape architect Capability Brown, and certainly the design, with its circuit ride, lake, canals and picturesque buildings including a ruin, a hermitage, a *momento mori* bridge and a bathhouse, are typical of his work. The bathhouse is the only one of these buildings to have survived, converted into a cottage now called The Summer House.

As a bathhouse, the building probably consisted of the decorated facade fronting a room for enjoying the view and taking tea, and a semi-subterranean room below housing the bath itself. The building still straddles a ditch that passes beneath it through stone arches, and on special occasions William opens a sluice allowing water to flow along it as it once did in order to feed the bath. As soon as fresh water bathing in the privacy of your own grotto became outmoded, the bathhouse would have been left to crumble like the other follies on the estate. Instead, it was preserved when, due to a series of deaths in the Clanricarde family at the beginning of the 19th century, there were two dowagers requiring a home. One was given an

LEFT On the lower ground floor, accessed downstairs from the entrance hall or through the lower doorway beneath the outside steps, there is a charmingly rustic kitchen. The glazed door on the right leads out to a small terrace above the canal, which is usually dry but can be filled with water, again by the operation of a sluice gate.

BELOW Despite being a room of very modest proportions, the kitchen enjoys the luxury of two sinks: one stone, found lying in the grass, now set into a wooden surface with curtained cupboards beneath; the other set into the top of an 18th-century French sideboard. The floor is laid with reclaimed terracotta tiles.

existing house, the other was given the former bathhouse, modifed to make a small, elegant residence with a new extension at the back and an upper storey.

After the death of dowager Urania, the 12th Countess, the cottage was demoted to house head gardeners on the estate. By the second half of the 20th century it had been unoccupied for some years and was falling into ruin, its predicament advertised by its inclusion in the catalogue for the 1974 exhibition at the Victoria and Albert Museum,

'The Destruction of the English Country House'. Six years later it was at last rescued from dereliction by a local couple who bought it very cheaply, re-roofed it and made it habitable again. What they could not afford to do was restore it to its former aesthetic glory. This stage of the building's renaissance fell to William Thuillier and his American friend Robert Perkins, who happened to be looking for a weekend cottage on the South Coast where they could stay when they went surfing. 'It was a bit of a mess, but Bob said he thought

he might buy it, and I said that if he decided not to, then I would, so we bought it together,' William relates.

Sound, but reduced in charm with plywood doors, strip lighting and a complete lack of internal architectural features, the cottage could not have found more dedicated new owners. Robert, who died in 1992 only seven years after they bought it, was an interior decorator, and William is a Bond Street art dealer, specializing in 17th- and 18th-century paintings. Between them they transformed the cottage from an attractive shell with a disappointing interior into a jewel box of a house.

LEFT Also on the lower ground floor, this bedroom has a door leading out onto a terrace over the canal on the opposite side of the building from the kitchen. Victorian needlework pictures hang above the bed and the occasional chair on the right has carved gothic detail.

RIGHT The central room on this floor is still a bathroom, although with all the comforts of heated water and modern plumbing. In the 18th century it would probably have been decorated as a grotto, possibly embellished with shells and pebbles, a look that William has plans to revive by 'grottifying' the room, as he calls it.

Their most important find was an excellent local joiner, Lionel Daniels of Froxfield. 'Even Bob, who was an absolute perfectionist, approved of his work,' says William. Working to designs from the period, Lionel Daniels made new glazing bars for the windows, architraves, panelled doors and a steep little staircase that rises from the entrance hall. Robert found fireplaces for the three reception rooms on the ground floor and for the bedrooms, and appropriate cornicing was installed. More recently, William laid oak floorboards in the reception rooms and re-glazed the front door in a design of octagons copied from an illustration of a late 18th-century *cottage orné* that he spotted in an issue of *Country Life* magazine.

As a first-time visitor, you would never guess that this pretty period piece was not entirely original. Its layout is delightful. The new glazed door at the top of the stone stairs opens into a barrel-vaulted hall. Ahead there is a small, square inner hall with a door on the right and one on the left. Through the door on the right is the more formal of the two small sitting rooms, its far wall having just enough space for a charming gothic chimney piece, with a pair of spiky gothic chairs on either side. The door on the left leads into an identically proportioned room with a different fireplace and a banquette tucked into a

corner. In between these two rooms, and entered from each through a slim gothic arch, is the central octagonal room, which occupies the front bay of the facade and sits directly above the room where the bath itself was situated. Here, the shape of the room is echoed by an octagonal table, although there is only space for six chairs around it.

Much of the appeal of this trio of rooms derives from the discrepancy between floor space and the relative grandeur of the architecture and furnishings. It is as if a capacious rectory or even a modest stately home had been shrunk and most of its contents squeezed out. Ceilings are high, windows tall, the doors glossy mahogany, the carved chimney pieces

ABOVE The two upstairs bedrooms lost height when the ceilings below were raised and their arched gothic windows now reach almost down to the floor. The chimney piece is one of several antique examples found by Robert Perkins for the house. The set of painted Regency chairs displays a particularly amusing interpretation of gothic ornament.

RIGHT The stairs leading down
to the entrance hall can be glimpsed
through the open door of the same
bedroom. A tiny bathroom is squeezed
between this room and the bedroom
on the other side of the landing.

BELOW Guests have a view from
their pillows of the canal and gardens
framed by chintz curtains. William
Thuillier is an art dealer, specializing in
17th- and 18th-century landscapes and
portraits, and all the rooms are hung
with a delightful selection of pictures
that are 'more pretty than valuable'.

beautifully detailed, and yet neither sitting room is big enough to accommodate as much as a three-seat sofa.

On the floors below and above, the ceilings are lower, the detailing more simple and the fireplaces smaller. The room that originally housed the bath is appropriately a bathroom. Next to it there is an old-fashioned kitchen with a floor of terracotta tiles and two sinks, one of which is stone and was found in the garden. On the other side of the bathroom is a bedroom, and there are two more bedrooms and a tiny bathroom upstairs.

William likes to get away to the cottage as often as possible. 'It's the perfect place to come and potter,' he says. And he always has plans for further improvements and embellishments to the place. Next on his list is to finish restoring the stone steps, and then perhaps some work on the stone quatrefoils.

ELEGANCE
finishing touches

- SYMMETRY Cottage rooms are often architecturally asymmetrical, but a symmetrical focal point, such as a mantelpiece, can be enough to introduce an air of elegant formality. Doris Urquhart's tiny bedroom mantelpiece immediately draws the eye with its pair of plates on either side of a jug and arrangement on the wall above of a mirror with matching candle sconces either side.

- PAIRS Buying things in pairs, whether lamps, cushions, plates or occasional chairs, is one way to ensure that you can create some symmetry. But you can still achieve the desired effect with things that do not match perfectly, as William Thuillier has in one of his bedrooms. Even though only the lamps and cushions are perfect pairs, the placing of pictures and furniture is attractively balanced.

- SCALE Small rooms do not necessarily benefit from small pieces of furniture. One large, handsome item such as a four-poster bed, a bookcase or a large painting, can make them seem bigger by conferring a certain grandeur. Binny Mathews has used carved and gilded French pelmets over cottage windows in her bedroom and study to charming effect.

- LIGHTING Overhead lighting is problematic in rooms with low ceilings. One solution that works particularly well in kitchens where good light is essential, is to install sunken spotlights. In other rooms where the modernity of a ceiling twinkling with halogen would jar, table and floor lamps, or wall lights are a better alternative.

- DINING Binny Mathews has a separate dining room, but many cottages don't have the space. Doris Urquhart has placed a metal chandelier hanging low over her kitchen table, fitted with candles. During the day the room has the informal feel of a working kitchen, but at night when the candles are lit the atmosphere is transformed for dining.

- RESTRAINT This is important in cottages with small rooms and low ceilings. Plain walls and fabrics make a calm background for furnishings, and painting the interior of a house the same colour throughout has the effect of making it seem more spacious. Doris Urquhart has gone one step further, painting all walls, ceilings and woodwork in the same shade of pink.

- CHECKS AND STRIPES As elegant relief from plain colours, you cannot do better than a ticking stripe. George Carter bought the fabric for his sitting room curtains very cheaply from a local draper and enlivens the plain walls in a bedroom with striped bed linen. Checks and stripes work well together, as used by both George Carter and Doris Urquhart.

- PICTURES Close-hung pictures in matching frames, whether photographs, photocopies or watercolour sketches, as in one of George Carter's bedrooms, always look smart.

DIRECTORY OF UK & US SOURCES

Every owner cites antique shops, centres, markets and fairs, auction houses, boot fairs and even charity shops as sources for many, if not most, of their furnishings. These would be far too numerous to mention in total and you doubtless have your own local favourites.

ARCHITECTURAL SALVAGE

LASSCO
Brunswick House
30 Wandsworth Road
London SW8 2LG
+44 (0)20 7394 2100
www.lassco.co.uk
One of the best, with a huge stock of everything from fireplaces to floors to stained glass, panelling and staircases, plus a very authentic range of replicas.

ORIGINAL ARCHITECTURAL ANTIQUES COMPANY
Ermin Farm, Cricklade Road
Cirencester
Gloucestershire GL7 5PN
+44 (0)1285 869222
www.originaluk.com
Reclaimed oak beams for ceilings and above fireplaces, plus a good selection of fireplaces and limestone troughs.

WALCOT RECLAMATION
108 Walcot Street
Bath BA1 5BG
+44 (0)1225 444404
www.walcot.com
Extensive stock including traditional building materials and architectural antiques, plus reproduction items.

ARCHITECTURAL ACCENTS
2711 Piedmont Road NE
Atlanta, GA 30305
(+1) 404 266 8700
www.architectural accents.com
Antique light fixtures, door hardware, garden antiques and other reclaimed items.

SALVAGE ONE
Architectural Salvage Company
1524 South Sangamon
Chicago, IL 60608
(+1) 312 733 0098
www.salvageone.com
Architectural artifacts.

BATHROOMS

ANTIQUE BATHS OF IVYBRIDGE
Erme Bridge Works
Ermington Road, Ivybridge
Devon PL21 9DE
+44 (0)1752 698250
www.antiquebaths.com
Excellent range of reconditioned antique baths, plus reproduction ranges.

CATCHPOLE & RYE
Saracens Dairy, Jobs Lane
Pluckley, Kent TN24 OSA
+44 (0)1233 840840
www.crye.co.uk
Antique and reproduction sanitaryware.

C.P. HART
+44 (0)20 7902 5250
www.cphart.co.uk
Inspiring showrooms for kitchens as well as bathrooms.

STIFFKEY BATHROOMS
89 Upper St Giles Street
Norwich NR2 1AB
+44 (0)1603 627850
www.stiffkeybathrooms.com
Antique sanitaryware and their own range of period and bespoke bathroom accessories.

THE WATER MONOPOLY
16–18 Lonsdale Road
London NW6 6RD
+44 (0)20 7624 2636
www.watermonopoly.com
Opulent period baths, basins and fittings.

SIGNATURE HARDWARE
2700 Crescent Springs Pike
Erlanger KY 41017
(+1) 866 855 2284
www.clawfootsupply.com
Complete supply of authentic reproduction clawfoot tubs, pedestal and console sinks, Topaz copper soaking tubs and more.

VINTAGE PLUMBING
(+1) 818 772 1721
www.vintageplumbing.com
Original and restored to perfection bathroom antiques, including pull-chain toilets and clawfoot bathtubs.

BLINDS

TIDMARSH
+44 (0)1279 401960
www.tidmarsh.co.uk
All types of blind, including wooden Venetian blinds.

FABRICS

ANNABEL GREY FABRICS
+44 (0)7748 742150
www.annabelgrey.co.uk
Gorgeous designs with a vintage feel, suitable for curtains, blinds and cushions.

ANTA
+44 (0)1862 832477
www.anta.co.uk
Plaids and checks in colours inspired by the Scottish landscape.

BENNISON FABRICS
16 Holbein Place
London SW1W 8NL
+44 (0)20 7730 8076
www.bennisonfabrics.com
Tea-stained chintzes, faded florals, stripes and damasks in gentle colours for a look of faded elegance.

CHELSEA TEXTILES
13 Walton Street
London SW3 2HX
+44 (0)20 7584 5544
www.chelseatextiles.com
Gorgeous embroidered cottons, delicate prints, linens, silks and voiles with a distinctly 18th-century feel.

COLEFAX AND FOWLER
110 Fulham Road
London SW3 6HU
+44 (0)20 7244 7427
+44 (0)20 8874 6484 for stockists
www.colefax.com
Quintessentially English fabrics and wallpapers.

DESIGNERS GUILD
+44 (0)20 7351 5775
www.designersguild.com
Fresh, pretty designs for curtains and upholstery.

IAN MANKIN
109 Regents Park Road
London NW1 8UR
+44 (0)20 7722 0997
www.ianmankin.co.uk
Huge range of natural fabrics, including unbleached linens, butter muslin and striped tickings.

LEWIS & WOOD
Woodchester Mill
North Woodchester
Stroud
Gloucestershire GL5 5NN
+44 (0)1453 878517
www.lewisandwood.co.uk
Gloriously eccentric wallpapers and fabrics, including engravings of ships, 18th-century-style hunting and fishing scenes, plus more traditional designs.

MELIN TREGWYNT
Castlemorris
Haverfordwest SA62 5UX
+44 (0)1348 891644
www.melintregwynt.co.uk
Cosy woven blankets, upholstery fabrics, throws and cushions combining traditional skills with innovative, modern designs.

OSBORNE & LITTLE
+44 (0)20 7352 1456 (UK)/(+1) 203 359 1500 (US)
www.osborneandlittle.com
Fabrics and trimmings to suit all tastes and styles of interior.

RUSSELL & CHAPPLE
23 Monmouth Street
London WC2H 9DE
+44 (0)20 7836 7521
www.randc.net
Artist's canvas in various weights, jutes, fine muslin, deckchair canvas and hessian sacking.

ST JUDES
+44 (0)1263 587666 for stockists
www.stjudesgallery.co.uk
Artist-designed vintage-feel textiles.

SANDERSON
+44 (0)1423 500051
www.sandersonfabrics.co.uk
Reproductions of William Morris fabrics and wallpapers.

LAURA ASHLEY, INC.
www.lauraashley.com
www.lauraashley-usa.com
for your nearest branch.
English-garden-look floral, striped, checked, and solid cotton fabrics for every room in the house. Coordinated pillows, bedding, wallpaper and trims.

SCALAMANDRÉ
(+1) 212 980 3888
www.scalamandre.com
for your nearest showroom.
Opulent fabrics from around the world to lend your home a globetrotter look.

ANTIQUE FABRICS

BEYOND FRANCE
www.beyondfrance.co.uk
Online shop with a large range of vintage linens, including monogrammed Hungarian grain and flour sacks and Romanian checked throws and tablecloths.

JANE SACCHI LINENS
+44 (0)20 7351 3160
www.janesacchi.com
Antique French linens including mattress tickings and monogrammed bedlinen.

PAVILION ANTIQUES
Church House
29 Church Street
Bradford-on-Avon
Wilts BA15 1LN
+44 (0)1225 866136 for an appointment
Specialists in antique French linens, with hemp sheeting, mattress tickings, also bedhangings, curtains and domestic linens.

TALENT FOR TEXTILES
+44 (0)1225 866 136
Runs antique textiles fairs throughout the West Country, bringing together dealers from all over the country in a series of attractive locations. Telephone for details.

FITTINGS

CLAYTON MUNROE
+44 (0)1803 865700
www.claytonmunroe.com
*Traditional French handles, a 'Celtic'
range and country-style aged iron hinges
and latches, available mail order only.*

JIM LAWRENCE
The Ironworks
Lady Lane Industrial Estate
Hadleigh, Suffolk IP7 6BQ
+44 (0)1473 86680
www.jim-lawrence.co.uk
*Ironwork with a hand-forged feel from
curtain poles and door handles to lighting
and furniture, plus soft furnishings.*

FURNITURE – contemporary

HABITAT
www.habitat.net for your nearest store
*Accessible contemporary furnishings at
accessible prices.*

IKEA
+44 (0)845 3552262 (UK)/(+1) 800 434
4532 (US) www.ikea.com for your
nearest store
Good design, piled high and sold cheap.

LIGNE ROSET
www.ligne-roset.com
Sleek modern furnishings.

OKA
+44 (0)20 7590 9895 for branches
+44 (0)844 815 7380 for mail order
www.okadirect.com
*Good quality, mid price furnishings in
classic contemporary and traditional styles.*

ANTHROPOLOGIE
www.anthropologie.com
for your nearest store
*Offer vintage-inspired one-of-a-kind home
accessories and decorative details.*

CRATE & BARREL
www.crateandbarrel.com
for your nearest store
Contemporary furniture and accessories.

FURNITURE – antique, vintage and traditional

ASPACE
+44 (0)845 8722400
www.aspace.co.uk
*Mail order furniture for children,
including stripey bedlinen.*

ACORN ANTIQUES
39 High Street
Dulverton
Somerset TA22 9DW
+44 (0)1398 323286
www.acornantiquesexmoor.co.uk
*Antiques plus handmade Chesterfield,
Knole and Howard sofas to order.*

AFTER NOAH
261 King's Road
London SW3 5EL
+44 (0)20 7351 2610
www.afternoah.com
*An appealing mix of antique, vintage,
and contemporary furnishings, including
cast iron beds, lighting and toys.*

BED BAZAAR
The Old Station, Station Road
Framlingham
Suffolk IP13 9EE
+44 (0)1728 723756
www.bedbazaar.co.uk
*Antique metal and wooden beds and
hand-made mattresses to order.*

JOANNA BOOTH ANTIQUES
PO Box 50886
London SW3 5YH
+44 (0)20 7352 8998 for an appointment
www.joannabooth.co.uk
*Early, and rare antiques including
sculpture and tapestries.*

LEIGH EXTENCE
55 High Street
Devon EX14 1ZL
+44 (0)1395 446830
www.extence.co.uk
*Antique clocks including that English
essential, the grandfather clock.*

LLOYD LOOM
Unit 59
Childerditch Hall Farm
Childerditch
Essex CM13 3HD
+44 (0)1277 812777
www.lloyd-loom-furniture.co.uk
*New versions of the ubiquitous and
loveable furnishings made from weaving
twisted paper and wire.*

MARGARET HOWELL
34 Wigmore Street
London W1U 2RS
+44 (0)20 7009 9006
www.margarethowell.co.uk
*Twentieth-century British design classics
from Ercol to Anglepoise, new and old.*

THE ODD CHAIR COMPANY
535 King's Road
London SW10 0SZ
+44 (0)20 7352 4700
+44 (0)1772 691777 for brochure
www.theoddchaircompany.com
*Traditional and unusual chairs, sofas,
both antique and reproduction.*

TALISMAN
79–91 New Kings Road
London SW6 4SQ
+44 (0)20 7731 4686
www.talisman-antiques.co.uk
Inspiring mix of unusual antiques.

WALKER RESTORATION
+44 (0)1406 363609
www.walkerrestoration.co.uk
*Online shop selling recycled, handmade
painted furniture.*

CLINTON HOWELL ANTIQUES
150 East 72nd Street
New York, NY 10021
(+1) 212 517 5879
www.clintonhowell.com
*English and continental furniture from
the 17th to the 20th centuries.*

FLOORING

**ALTERNATIVE FLOORING
COMPANY**
+44 (0)1264 335111 for your
nearest stockist
www.alternativeflooring.com
*Coir, sea-grass, sisal, jute and wool floor
coverings.*

BERNARD DRU OAK
Bickham Manor, Timberscombe
Minehead, Somerset TA24 7UA
+44 (0)1643 841312
www.oakfloor.co.uk
*Specialists in oak flooring, cut from the
company's own Exmoor woodlands.*

CRUCIAL TRADING
+44 (0)1562 743747
www.crucial-trading.com
*All types of natural floorings, most of
which can also be ordered as rugs bound
with cotton, linen or leather.*

DELABOLE SLATE
Pengelly Road, Delabole
Cornwall PL33 9AZ
+44 (0)1840 212242
www.delaboleslate.co.uk
*Riven slate or slate slabs suitable for
work surfaces, fireplaces and flooring.*

ROGER OATES DESIGN
+44 (0)1531 632718 for stockists
www.rogeroates.com
*All kinds of natural floorings, including
chunky abaca, plus flat weave rugs and
runners in subtle stripes and felt matting.*

RUSH MATTERS
The Grange, Grange Farm
Colesden, Bedfordshire
+44 (0)1234 376419
www.rushmatters.co.uk
*Rush matting made with English rushes,
also baskets, and rush seating for chairs.*

**THE NATURAL WOOD FLOOR
COMPANY**
20 Smugglers Way
London SW18 1EQ
+44 (0)20 8871 9771
www.naturalwoodfloor.co.uk
Solid and parquet wood block flooring.

HEATING

BISQUE
244 Belsize Road
London NW6 4BT
+44 (0)20 7328 2225
www.bisque.co.uk
Suppliers of classic, fine radiators.

CHESNEYS
+44 (0)20 7267 1410 (UK)/
(+1) 646 840 0609 (US) for your
nearest stockist
www.chesneys.co.uk
*Huge range of modern and antique
fireplaces.*

**ARCHITECTURAL PANELING,
INC.**
(+1) 212 371 9632
www.apaneling.com
*Reproduction fireplaces, panelling
and mouldings.*

FINISHING TOUCHES

ABIGAIL AHERNE
137 Upper Street
London N1 1QP
+44 (0)20 7354 8181
www.atelierabigailahern.com
*Eccentric and unusual furniture,
wallpaper, lighting, ceramics and
textiles by artist-designers.*

FOURTH FORGE
Brown's Farmyard
Nettlecombe, Dorset DT6 3SS
+44 (0)1308 485099
www.fourthforge.co.uk
Hand-forged ironwork.

GRAHAM & GREEN
4 Elgin Crescent
London W11 2HX
+44 (0)20 7243 8908
mail order +44 (0)845 1306622
www.grahamandgreen.co.uk
*Glamorous and quirky glass, cushions,
tableware, lighting and a small range
of furniture including leather.*

LUSH DESIGNS
6a Greenwich Market
Greenwich, London SE10 9HZ
+44 (0)20 8293 5662
www.lushlampshades.co.uk
*Bold, beautifully drawn patterns
featuring animals and plants on cushions,
tea towels and lampshades, with a distinctly
English, slightly primitive charm.*

MADE IN CLEY
Starr House, High Street
Cley, Holt NR25 7RF
+44 (0)1263 740134
www.madeincley.co.uk
*Locally made ceramics, including
porcelain, earthenware and raku.*

PAPA STOUR
www.papastour.com
Online Scottish designs.

SETH CARDEW
Masia Albadas
12164 Rosildos
Castellon, Spain
(+ 34) 964 706809
www.wenfordbridge.com
Gorgeous painted pottery.

KITCHENS

AGA RAYBURN
+44 (0)8457 125207
www.agarayburn.co.uk
Classic cast-iron heat storage cookers.

FIRED EARTH
+44 (0)845 3660400 for brochure and
stores nationwide
www.firedearth.com
*Kitchens, bathrooms and tiles, also
an excellent range of paint colours.*

PLAIN ENGLISH
Stowupland Hall, Stowupland
Stowmarket, Suffolk IP14 4BE
+44 (0)1449 774028
+44 (0)870 240 3562 for brochure
www.plainenglishdesign.co.uk
*Elegant, simple wooden kitchens suitable
for traditional and period interiors.*

SMEG
+44 (0)844 557907 for stockists
www.smeguk.com
*Stainless steel kitchen appliances and
retro style fridges in a range of colours.*

CROWN POINT CABINETRY
153 Charlestown Road
Claremont, NH 03743
(+1) 800 999 4994
www.crown-point.com
Custom cabinets for kitchen and bath.

PAINT

PAPERS AND PAINTS
+44 (0)20 7352 8626
www.paper-paints.co.uk
*As well as their excellent range of paints,
this company mixes any colour to order.*

FARROW & BALL
www.farrow-ball.com
*Unbeatable for subtle paint colours with
strange names, papers, varnishes & stains.*

FRANCESCA'S PAINTS
+44 (0)20 7228 7694
www.francescaspaint.com
*Traditional limewash, eco emulsion
paint & chalky emulsion.*

THE LITTLE GREENE PAINT
COMPANY
+44 (0)845 8805855
www.thelittlegreene.com
Quality paint in a large range of colours.

THE PAINT LIBRARY
+44 (0)20 7823 7755
www.paintlibrary.co.uk
*Excellent quality paint and wallpaper
including innumerable shades of
off-white.*

DEFINE BY DESIGN
(+1) 817 845 9558
www.definebydesign.com
Faux and decorative finishes.

JANOVIC
(+1) 800 772 4381
www.janovic.com for your nearest store
*Quality paints from a wide variety
of makers.*

LIGHTING

CHAPLINS
477–507 Uxbridge Road
Hatch End
Pinner
Middlesex HA5 4JS
+44 (0)20 8421 1779
www.chaplins.co.uk
*Good range of chic modern furnishings
and lighting including Marcel Wanders'
'Big Shadow Lamp' for Cappellini.*

VAUGHAN
+44 (0)20 7349 4600 for stockists
www.vaughandesigns.com
*Wide range of replica period lighting
from lamps to sconces to chandeliers.*

ANTIQUE LIGHTING COMPANY
8214 Greenwood Avenue North
Seattle, WA 98103
(+1) 800 224 7880
www.antiquelighting.com
*Replicas of beautiful antique fixtures
and custom lighting.*

VICTORIAN REVIVAL
(+1) 416 789 1704
www.victorian-revival.com
*Online purveyor of architectural antiques,
including wall sconces, hanging fixtures,
floor lamps and porch lights.*

WALLCOVERINGS

LEWIS & WOOD
(see also under Fabrics)
www.lewisandwood.co.uk

DE GOURNAY
+44 (0)20 7352 9988 (UK)/(+1) 212 564
9750 (US) for your nearest stockist
www.degournay.com
*Reproductions of hand-painted 18th
century Chinese wallpapers – perhaps
a bit grand for most cottages.*

OUTDOORS

BENNETTS TRADITIONAL
MARQUEES
3 Riviera Court
Suffolk Road
Bournemouth
Dorset BH2 5SY
+44 (0)1202 622622
www.bennettsmarquees.co.uk
*Manufacture, repair and hire of
marquees.*

CREDITS

KEY: ph=photographer, a=above, b=below, r=right, l=left, c=centre.

All photography by Jan Baldwin unless otherwise stated below

Front jacket Caroline Zoob, designer/thank you to The National Trust, Monk's House, Rodmell, Lewes, Sussex – please check website for details: www.nationaltrust.org.uk; endpapers ph Jerry Harpur; page 1 owner of Westcott Design, Peter Westcott's cottage in Somerset; 2 Stephen & Clare Pardy's house in Suffolk; 3 Philip & Lisskulla Wagner's cottage in Sussex designed by Philip Wagner Architects; 4–5 owner of Westcott Design, Peter Westcott's cottage in Somerset; 6 Caroline Zoob, designer/thank you to The National Trust, Monk's House, Rodmell, Lewes, Sussex – please check website for details: www.nationaltrust.org.uk; 7a Jane Moran's cottage in Sussex; 7b Philip & Lisskulla Wagner's cottage in Sussex designed by Philip Wagner Architects; 8 Doris Urquhart & Christopher Richardson; 9 artist Binny Mathews & architect Stuart Martin's home in Dorset; 10 Jane Moran's cottage in Sussex; 11 owner of Girl's Own Store, Sara Mahon's cottage in West Dorset; 12–13 Caroline Zoob, designer/thank you to The National Trust, Monk's House, Rodmell, Lewes, Sussex – please check website for details: www.nationaltrust.org.uk; 14–23 owner of Westcott Design, Peter Westcott's cottage in Somerset; 24–29 Caroline Zoob, designer/thank you to The National Trust, Monk's House, Rodmell, Lewes, Sussex – please check website for details: www.nationaltrust.org.uk; 30–37 owner of Girl's Own Store, Sara Mahon's cottage in West Dorset; 38al, ar & br owner of Westcott Design, Peter Westcott's cottage in Somerset; 38bl owner of Girl's Own Store, Sara Mahon's cottage in West Dorset; 39a & c Caroline Zoob, designer/thank you to The National Trust, Monk's House, Rodmell, Lewes, Sussex – please check website for details: www.nationaltrust.org.uk; 39b owner of Westcott Design, Peter Westcott's cottage in Somerset; 40–41 Malcolm & Anna Seal's cottage in West Dorset; 42–51 Jane Moran's cottage in Sussex; 52–61 Charlotte Molesworth, artist, gardener & flower arranger, cottage in Weald of Kent; 62–71 all Françoise Price's & Gerry Peachey's cottage in Wiltshire except for 62al © Ari Ashley – Ari Ashley's shepherd's hut; 72–77 Malcolm & Anna Seal's cottage in West Dorset; 78a & c Françoise Price's & Gerry Peachey's cottage in Wiltshire; 78b Malcolm & Anna Seal's cottage in West Dorset; 79l both Charlotte Molesworth, artist, gardener & flower arranger, cottage in Weald of Kent; 79ar Françoise Price's & Gerry Peachey's cottage in Wiltshire; 79cr Jane Moran's cottage in Sussex; 79br Malcolm & Anna Seal's cottage in West Dorset; 80–81 Elizabeth Machin's Norfolk cottage; 82–91 Philip & Lisskulla Wagner's cottage in Sussex designed by Philip Wagner Architects; 92–99 Rose Bamford of Dandy Star's home in Cornwall; 100–105 Elizabeth Machin's Norfolk cottage; 106a ph Paul Massey: 106c ph Paul Massey/Hotel Tresanton, St Mawes, Cornwall owned and designed by Olga Polizzi; 106b Philip & Lisskulla Wagner's cottage in Sussex designed by Philip Wagner Architects; 107al Elizabeth Machin's Norfolk cottage; 107bl ph Paul Massey/Hotel Tresanton, St Mawes, Cornwall owned and designed by Olga Polizzi; 107ar Rose Bamford of Dandy Star's home in Cornwall; 107br Philip & Lisskulla Wagner's cottage in Sussex designed by Philip Wagner Architects; 108–117 antique dealers Robert Hirschhorn's & John Hall's home in London; 118–125 Cressida Granger of Mathmos' cottage in Dorset; 126–133 Stephen & Clare Pardy's house in Suffolk; 134–143 the Suffolk home of Katie Fontana, creative director of Plain English; 144l both Cressida Granger of Mathmos' cottage in Dorset; 144ar antique dealers Robert Hirschhorn's & John Hall's home in London; 144br Stephen & Clare Pardy's house in Suffolk; 145a Malcolm & Anna Seal's cottage in West Dorset; 145c Cressida Granger of Mathmos' cottage in Dorset; 145b Stephen & Clare Pardy's house in Suffolk; 146–147 Doris Urquhart & Christopher Richardson; 148–157 artist Binny Mathews & architect Stuart Martin's home in Dorset; 158–167 Doris Urquhart & Christopher Richardson; 168–173 George Carter's cottage in Norfolk; 174–183 William Thuillier's folly in Hampshire; 184a & c Doris Urquhart & Christopher Richardson; 184b George Carter's cottage in Norfolk; 185al artist Binny Mathews & architect Stuart Martin's home in Dorset; 185bl Doris Urquhart & Christopher Richardson; 185ar William Thuillier's folly in Hampshire; 185br George Carter's cottage in Norfolk.

Architects, designers and
business owners whose
work is featured in this book:

BINNY MATHEWS

www.hereasel.com
Binny's portrait-commissioning website
+44 (0)1935 83455
Stuart Martin
stuart@stuartmartinarchitects.com
+44 (0)1935 83543
Pages 9, 148–157, 185al

CAROLINE ZOOB

Designer
www.carolinezoob.com
+44 (0)1273 479274
Front jacket, pages 6, 12–13, 24–29, 39a, 39c

CHARLOTTE MOLESWORTH

Artist, gardener and flower arranger
charlotte@cdmolesworth.co.uk
Pages 52–61, 79l both

DANDY STAR

www.dandystar.com
mail@dandystar.com
+44 (0)20 7923 7208
+44 (0)1840 250909
Pages 92–99, 107ar

DORIS URQUHART AND
CHRISTOPHER RICHARDSON
ANTIQUES

www.antiquesatbartholomew.co.uk
+44 (0)7799 414505
*Pages 8, 146–147, 158–167, 184a,
184,c, 185bl*

ELIZABETH MACHIN INTERIORS PR

emachin@blueyonder.co.uk
+44 (0)20 7503 3200
Pages 80–81, 100–105, 107al

GEORGE CARTER

Norfolk cottage available to rent
grcarter@easynet.co.uk
+44 (0)1362 668130
Pages 168–173, 184b, 185br

GIRL'S OWN STORE

30 South Street
Bridport
Dorset DT6 3NQ
www.girlsownstore.co.uk
+44 (0)1308 424474
Pages 11, 30–37, 38bl

HOTEL TRESANTON

(Olga Polizzi – owner and
interior designer)
St Mawes
Cornwall TR2 5DR
www.tresanton.com
+44 (0)1326 270055
Pages 106c, 107bl

MALCOLM SEAL

Basket maker and gardener
www.malcolmseal.co.uk
+44 (0)1308 485515
pages 40–41, 72–77, 78b, 79br, 145a

MATHMOS

www.mathmos.com
+44 (0)20 7549 2700
Pages 118–125, 144l both , 145c

MONK'S HOUSE –
THE NATIONAL TRUST

Rodmell, Lewes
Sussex BN7 3HF
Please check the website for details:
www.nationaltrust.org.uk
Front jacket, pages 6, 12–13, 24–29, 39a, 39c

PHILIP WAGNER ARCHITECTS

Architecture, planning and
interior design
5 Ladbroke Road
London W11 3PA
www.philipwagner.co.uk
mailbox@philipwagner.co.uk
+44 (0)20 7221 3219
Pages 3, 7b, 82–91, 106b, 107br

PLAIN ENGLISH

www.plainenglishdesign.co.uk
+44 (0)1449 774028
Pages 134–143

ROBERT HIRSCHHORN
ANTIQUES

Early oak and country furniture
and distinctive period objects
London by appointment
www.hirschhornantiques.com
info@hirschhornantiques.com
+44 (0)20 7703 7443
+44 (0)7831 405937
Pages 108–117, 144ar

SHEPHERD'S HUT
RESTORATION COMPANY

www.shepherdshuts.co.uk
fgl@pricepeachey.fsnet.co.uk
+44 (0)1249 701439
Pages 62–71, 78a 78c, 79ar

STEPHEN PARDY

Weston Pardy Design Consultancy
49 Cleaver Square
London SE11 4EA
weston.pardy@mac.com
+44 (0)20 7587 0221
Pages 2, 126–133, 144br, 145b

WESTCOTT DESIGN LTD

www.westcott-design.com
peter@westcott-design.com
+44 (0)20 7801 0072
Pages 1, 4–5, 14–23, 38al, 38ar, 38br, 39b

WILLIAM THUILLIER

European paintings 1600–1850
14 Old Bond Street
London W1S 4PP
www.thuillart.com
thuillart@aol.com
+44 (0)20 7499 0106
David Mendel – painted finishes
Lionel Daniel – joinery
de Gournay – dining room wallpaper
Pages 174–183, 185ar

INDEX
Page numbers in *italic* refer to illustrations and their captions

ACKNOWLEDGMENTS

I would like to thank everyone at Ryland Peters & Small who has contributed to the production of this book and in particular Alison Starling, Leslie Harrington, Toni Kay, Emily Westlake, Delphine Lawrance and Clare Double. It was a great pleasure to work with photographer Jan Baldwin whose pictures so elegantly capture the atmosphere and style of each location. I would also like to thank my father George Byam Shaw who supplied the poetry, Miranda Eden who suggested two excellent houses for the book, and all the house owners who so generously opened their doors, gave their time and shared their ideas. Lastly, I am as always grateful to my husband and co-driver for his unfailing support.